BEAD & FIBER JEWELRY

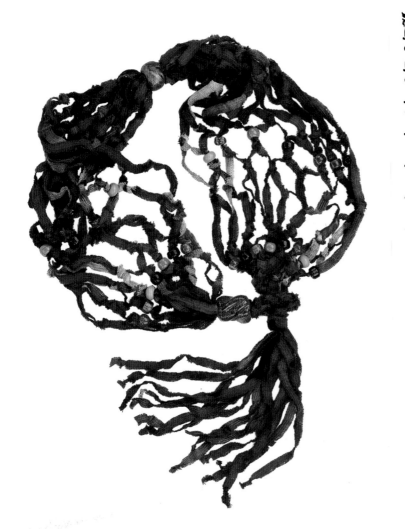

BEAD & FIBER JEWELRY

ELEGANT KNOTTED DESIGNS

Jane Olson-Phillips

A Division of Sterling Publishing Co., Inc.

New York / London

Senior Editor: Terry Taylor

Editor: Larry Shea

Assistant Editor: Mark Bloom

Art Director: Dana Irwin

Art Production: 828:design

Illustrator: Orrin Lundgren

Photographer: Stewart O'Shields

Cover Designer: Cindy LaBreacht

Library of Congress Cataloging-in-Publication Data

Olson-Phillips, Jane
Bead & fiber jewelry : elegant knotted designs / Jane Olson-Phillips. --1st ed.
    p. cm.
  Includes index.
  ISBN 978-1-60059-231-7 (pb-trade pbk. : alk. paper)
  1. Beadwork. 2. Fiberwork. 3. Jewelry making. I. Title.
  TT860.O57 2008
  745.594'2--dc22

                              2008005846

10 9 8 7 6 5 4 3 2 1

First Edition

Published by Lark Books, A Division of
Sterling Publishing Co., Inc.
387 Park Avenue South, New York, NY 10016

Text © 2008, Jane Olson-Phillips
Photography © 2008, Lark Books unless otherwise specified
Illustrations © 2008, Lark Books unless otherwise specified

Distributed in Canada by Sterling Publishing,
c/o Canadian Manda Group, 165 Dufferin Street
Toronto, Ontario, Canada M6K 3H6

Distributed in the United Kingdom by GMC Distribution Services,
Castle Place, 166 High Street, Lewes, East Sussex, England BN7 1XU

Distributed in Australia by Capricorn Link (Australia) Pty Ltd.,
P.O. Box 704, Windsor, NSW 2756 Australia

If you have questions or comments about this book, please contact:
Lark Books
67 Broadway
Asheville, NC 28801
828-253-0467

Manufactured in China

ISBN 13: 978-1-60059-231-7

For information about custom editions, special sales, premium and corporate purchases, please
contact Sterling Special Sales Department at 800-805-5489 or specialsales@sterlingpub.com.

BEAD & FIBER JEWELRY

Introduction

For me, it's all about the materials. I buy cords, threads, and yarns because I love fibers. I collect beads because I'm attracted to their colors, shapes, and surfaces. Most of all, I love how those very different materials are put together; I am fascinated with the way the textures and warmth of the fibers play against the hard, shiny surfaces of the beads to create something new and spectacular.

In this book, I'll show how to combine beads and fibers (two of the most popular art and craft materials) to create elegant pieces of wearable art that anyone can make. Forget any preconceived ideas you might have about knotting. And put aside thoughts of knotted rope hammocks or macramé plant hangers. Within these pages, I'll show you how to use five simple knots you use almost every day (even if you don't know their names). You'll learn a few new ways to use those knots, and how you can use them to transform ordinary fibers into jewelry you'll be proud to wear.

The skill levels of the projects in this book range from easy to advanced, and you'll learn something new in every single one of them. If you're new to knotting with beads, the first section of the book teaches you some of the techniques I've developed. You'll discover that you can use any type of fiber with any type of bead or stone you can think of. You

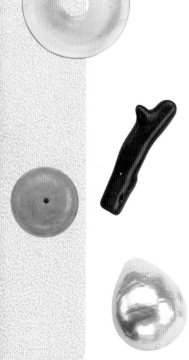

don't have to worry about threading the cord through the bead because I will show you ways to solve this problem.

If you've forgotten your summer camp knotting skills, the back of the book contains an illustrated how-to of all the knots used in the book. I suggest you dive right in with a simply elegant project like the easy-to-create Spiral Choker on page 22. You'll use just two knots to showcase a special bead of your choosing.

You'll also learn to use a wide variety of fibers: hemp, linen, silk, cotton, rayon, acrylic, and ribbon tape yarn. My bead selection ranges from antique to vintage to contemporary glass, silver, enamel, ceramic, bone, and even stones. If you like large old buttons, the Knot Just Buttons! Necklace (page 52) contains three large vintage buttons with three patterns that are the same size and color. Use round or square "donuts" in new ways with the Southwest Picot Choker (page 38) or with my personal favorite, Double Donuts (page 68). "Donuts" come in endless colors and sizes; they are fun to use. If you find a terrific stone that doesn't have a hole, don't worry! See the Black & White Necklace (page 44) and Drusy Stone Necklace (page 106) for elegant solutions to that little problem.

If you find some fiber you would like to use and don't have the perfect beads, you can use polymer clay to create your own.

I did! The Muted Multicolor Necklace (page 46), Netted Lariat Necklace (page 58), and Chunky Gold Net Necklace (page 86) all use beads I made myself.

The myriad ways you can combine beads and fibers are endless. I urge you to experiment, both while making the projects in this book and when you move on to create your own designs. Use different knots, other types of cords, beads that you've chosen to express your own tastes. I hope this book will start you on your way to creating one-of-a-kind jewelry. The new yet timeless art of knotting can spark your imagination and fulfill your jewelry desires for years.

Happy Knotting!

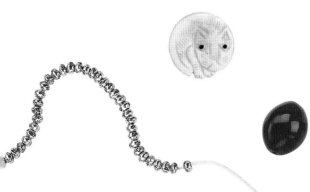

Jane Olson-Phillips
Azurite Brooch, 2007
2 1/2 x 4 inches (6.4 x 10.2 cm)
Linen and cotton cord, azurite cabochon, knitting needle, glass beads
Photo by Stewart O'Shields

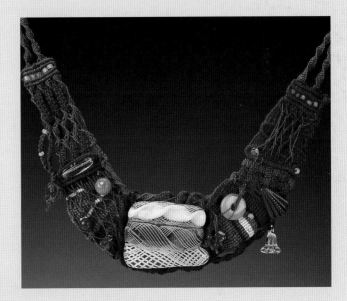

Jane Olson-Phillips
Red Linen Necklace, 2007
22 inches (55.9 cm)
Linen and cotton, fused glass, glass and stone beads
Photo by Stewart O'Shields

Bead & Fiber Basics
MATERIALS

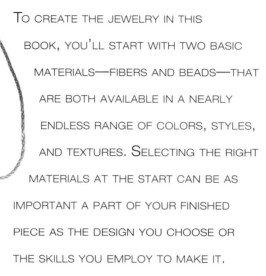

To create the jewelry in this book, you'll start with two basic materials—fibers and beads—that are both available in a nearly endless range of colors, styles, and textures. Selecting the right materials at the start can be as important a part of your finished piece as the design you choose or the skills you employ to make it.

FIBERS

Years ago, knotting or "macramé" was usually worked in linen, cotton, and jute. While linen and cotton are good choices, jute is too harsh and stiff for jewelry. Today we have many more choices, so be sure to select something friendly, something that won't fight you every step of the way. In this section, I've listed the fibers I've used to create the projects in this book.

By the way, "filler cords" add bulk to your knots, but they are usually not seen in a finished piece. If you are running short of a special cord when making your jewelry, you can use a different material for the filler cords.

Cotton

Cotton warp thread for weavers is a very strong cord, tightly twisted (as opposed to other cotton string). It comes in a very wide range of colors. In clove hitch knotting, cotton is only slightly softer then linen. Cotton and linen work well together—use linen for the filler cords, knotting over them with cotton.

Cotton Embroidery Floss

One of my favorite threads, cotton embroidery floss is easy to work with and comes in more than 150 colors. Although these threads aren't strong enough to use by themselves, you can knot them over filler cords. If you make a mistake with this floss, it is almost impossible to fix, so just cut it off and start again.

Crochet Cotton

Firm crochet cotton is another option. It works well knotted over other cords. If it is too soft, it becomes fuzzy and doesn't hold its shape. Foreign brands seem to be better quality.

Hemp

Hemp is noted for its strong fibers. Hemp cord used to be very rough and hard on the hands, but now it comes in a much smoother form and is less expensive than in the past. It comes in many colors and is great for children to use. When cutting cord lengths, though, check it over carefully before you use it, as it often has irregular bumps that you must cut out.

Linen

Linen is a fine, smooth cord, so don't use the waxed type. Five ply (the number refers to how many cords are twisted together) is very strong, but three ply also works well enough and makes a smaller knot. You can find small spools of linen cord in some thread departments. Larger spools are mostly used for upholstery and saddlery work. Linen cord typically comes in black, brown, blue, white, red, and natural.

Yarn

Silk, rayon, nylon, and acrylic yarns make good material for knotting if they are not too soft and flimsy. You can find multi-colored yarn and even yarn with metallic threads embedded. Try knotting a sample piece to see how they look and to make sure the knots will hold. If the ends start to fray, dab on some white glue and let it dry before knotting. You can also put glue on tassel ends or fringe if they start to unravel. You can burn some cords with a match to seal them.

Other Fibers

If you find a very thin metallic thread or another fiber you'd like to use, but think is too thin, you can combine it with another cord that you are already using. Just knot with the two cords together. This technique is also done in knitting and crochet.

BEADS

Beads are miniature treasures! There is an endless variety of bead materials available today: glass (old and new), metal, stone, plastic, polymer clay, and organic materials such as bone, horn, shell, amber, seeds, nuts, coral, pearls, and lots more.

Mixing beads with fibers is a way to create jewelry all your own. I never stop searching for interesting beads, buttons, and pendants. Many of my beads are too old and precious to use in my jewelry, but I always have plenty on hand to work with. Sometimes, it takes me a while to find the perfect fiber to match with them.

A bead can be the focal point of a jewelry piece, while the fiber in the background provides a contrast of texture against the bead's smooth shiny surface. The fiber can emphasize a specific color among the many in the bead. Even within the knots, smaller beads also do this. Alternately, the fiber can contrast the color of the bead.

Another way to look at the connection between the fiber and the bead is by examining the design and patterns of the knotting without a large focal bead. A large bead with a muted color or smaller beads can add to this design.

Stringing your beads on fiber helps to preserve and protect them. They don't have to hit against each other or be cut by wires. When storing your beads, keep your focal beads on a padded tray so you can see at a glance what you have available. Keep the more ordinary beads separated by color in trays or boxes. After you pick out a focal bead, select a tray or trays of the colors to choose from. Remember that all beads can be used in some way.

To measure your beads, you have to measure from hole to hole, not across the diameter. Bead catalogues have lots of useful information on sizes and materials.

MATCHING BEADS AND FIBERS

When you're working with beads and fibers, remember that one or the other should be dominant. If you study the pieces in this book, you should be able to see which dominates in each.

If you have a special focal bead, design your piece around it, with the fiber in the background carrying out the color theme. Don't choose brightly colored fibers that detract from the focal bead. Pick fibers that will echo the colors of the bead, but are slightly less intense.

If the fibers are dominant, use the knots to enhance the design and texture of the piece. Use the beads to augment and harmonize the colors. You don't need too many colors; pick a main one and no more than two others.

For examples of fiber dominance, see the Lacy Collar Necklace (page 55), Flower Brooch (page 95), Primary Colors Necklace (page 100), and Fiber Ruffle Necklace (page 104) projects. In this last project, the bright colors are dominant, but the focal bead brings it all together.

A color wheel can help you work with colors. For example, take a look at the Purple Pod Necklace on page 49. Since the pendant was a solid purple, I used an analogous color scheme on either side of the purple bead. The Primary Colors project uses colors equidistant on the color wheel from the focal color. The Flower Brooch is monochromatic—using one color with a slight amount of black on the bead as an accent. Whatever you do with color, be sure to take advantage of the many possibilities available and create a combination that works for you.

FASTENINGS

Besides your beads and fiber, you'll need fastenings to complete your necklaces. Luckily, there is an endless variety of fastenings for necklaces and bracelets. The most common are bolt rings, lobster clasps, and box clasps (which use a tongue-and-groove closure). They all have a loop through which you thread the fiber. If the loop is too small, you can still use the clasp. See Getting Started (page 16).

S hooks and figure-eight loops are easy to make from 16- to 18-gauge silver or gold-filled wire. Hammering the wire gives it a texture, if desired. You can even place a small bead in the middle of the "S." See the Fiber Ruffle Necklace on page 104.

Magnetic Clasps

Magnet clasps now come in several designs and sizes. They work well with fiber and are easy to use. While I can recommend them, there is nothing like the security of a physical loop and catch. Magnetic clasps are not my first choice for heavier necklaces.

Toggles

Toggles, like most fastenings, come in complementary pairs. One side is a ring, and the other side is a bar to push through it. Readily available in several metals, finishes, and sizes, toggles can be old or new, of various materials, and can match the color of your fiber. They can also make a statement, carrying the theme of your necklace.

In place of the standard toggle, you can use a flat button or disc bead on one side and a loop of knotted fiber on the other to catch the bead like a buttonhole. I particularly like using buttons with shanks. Buttons come in a variety of colors, as well as silver, gold, and pewter. I always keep a bunch on hand, ready to use. See Making a Loop (page 20).

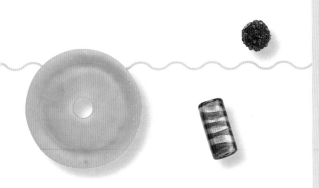

Polymer Clay

I mentioned making beads from polymer clay, but you can also use the material for toggles. It is easy to make a matching polymer clay button, bead, or even a fetish. See my fish toggles in the Ocean Wave Necklace (page 71) and Double Donuts (page 68). Also, see the matching toggle in the Funky Ceramic Bead Necklace (page 40).

You could even make a tag with your name on it. I find polymer clay offers a quick way to make a fastening, and if you don't have the right color clay, you can just paint it!

Hangers

Hangers are little metal disks that you can attach to a hole-less pendant or flat stone or glass disk. In fact, you can use hangers to hold any piece of jewelry. They are inexpensive double-holed discs about ⅚ inch (2.1 cm) long. You can bond the larger part to the flat surface of a hard object and run a cord or wire through the smaller hole. You can even attach two or three discs to one object if needed. See the Drusy Stone Necklace on page 106 for a sample.

Joan R. Babcock
Scallop Shell, 2007
11 x 3¾ inches (28 x 9.5 cm)
Nylon cord, copper, melon shell, glass beads
Photo by artist

Jane Olson-Phillips
Goddess Neck & Shoulder Piece, 2007
Linen and cotton cord, fused glass cab, glass goddesses, glass beads
Photo by Stewart O'Shields

TOOLS & EQUIPMENT

Knotting doesn't require a lot of tools besides your fingers. Once you dive in, you'll find you can carry your work with you anywhere.

BOARD—A "macramé board" is a soft 12 x 18-inch (30.5 x 45.7 cm) fiber board with a white grid and a plastic covering. These boards last forever and make your work easier, since you can pin your necklace in place as you work. The lines and measurements are helpful as guides. You can find them in craft catalogues. The basic size is large enough for any size necklace; however, you might also want a small board to knot earrings or bracelets on and to carry with you.

CARDBOARD—You'll need a flat surface to stick pins into. You can use the smooth side of heavy cardboard, although it can be a little hard to stick your pins in.

CORKBOARD—A small corkboard—the kind sold as a bulletin or pin-up board—is the best option as a surface for holding pins.

FILES—Small files of various shapes are handy for smoothing out a bead hole or getting rid of a sharp edge. Bead reamers—round, pointed files—are made especially for beads. You can buy them from bead-supply stores or catalogues.

GLUE—Use an industrial grade adhesive and sealant (a metal glue) for attaching findings or gluing metal pieces together. This glue must be bonded; to do this, put a small amount on both sides and allow them to dry to "tacky" before pressing them together. Allow the piece to set before continuing work. You should use fiber glue or white glue for sealing off ends or holding fibers together.

MAGNIFYING GLASS—Use one to get a close-up look at your knots. This can really be a big help when you need to untie a tangled knot.

NEEDLES—Tapestry needles have large holes to thread the cord through and blunt points so they don't hurt the fiber. Buy two or three different sizes. There are all sorts of uses for needles, like pulling cords through or underneath fibers. Note: You can also use a wire-beading needle for pulling a thin thread through a small hole in a bead.

PAPER—You'll need white sheets for sketching designs and lining your board. I recommend drawing a sketch or outline for each project. After drawing an outline for your work, you can tape it to your board and knot over it.

PINS—Use long straight pins with a knob on the end (also called "quilting pins"). You'll use pins throughout the knotting process to hold knots firm and in place.

RULER—Be sure to use a ruler that has both inches and centimeters. You'll need it to draw guidelines on paper and to ensure you have the needed length and width of materials. As you're making a project, you'll use one to check the lengths of knotted sections to make sure they're the size called for in the directions.

SCISSORS—You'll need small and very sharp scissors to cut close to the knots.

TAPE — You'll use transparent tape and masking tape, along with pins, to hold down the ends of a cord or a fastening when you start a project. A small piece of tape can hold the "tail" end while you tie a clove hitch, or it can hold cords out of the way when they are not needed. To help you pull a cord through a bead, cover the end in tape.

WIRE — Besides needles, I recommend having a thin piece of wire on hand— 4 inches (10 cm) long and bent in half—to thread larger amounts of cord. You'll find it necessary when you have too many threads or they are too wide for the needle.

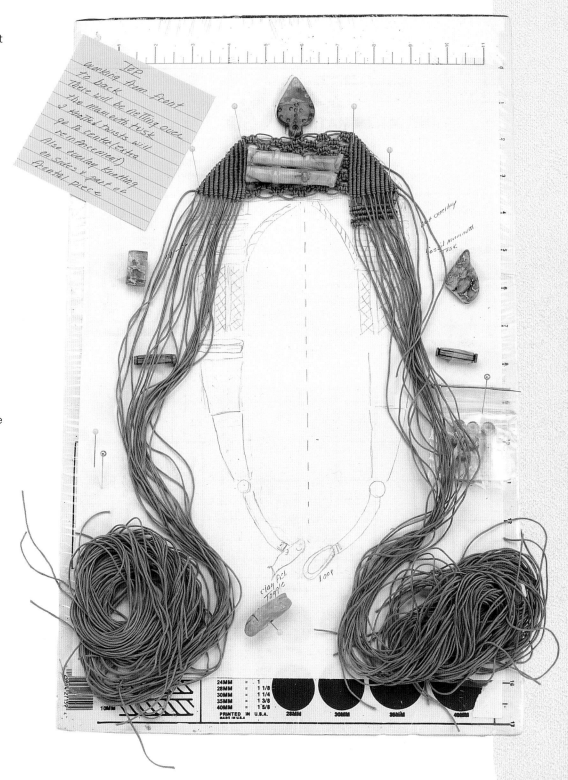

GETTING STARTED

This book presents 30 jewelry projects for you to work with. They run from basic chokers to more advanced work. Besides necklaces, you'll also find project instructions for bracelets, earrings, a purse, and two brooches. Each one offers new ideas, colors, textures, and beads. You will learn not only the knots, but also how they look and work with the various kinds of cords. As you work your way through the book, you'll gain experience in handling beads and fastenings. When you have mastered these projects, you will be ready to create your own jewelry.

The information in this section applies to my projects as well as to your own work. As you do the projects, remember that you can make them smaller or larger, change the fastenings, or swap the colors. Try to stay with the same fibers—the lengths are already worked out for you.

One more thing: As you work with the book's projects, examine the photos to see how each piece is laid out. This will help when you prepare to make it. Also, be sure to notice that I've marked the projects as easy, intermediate, or advanced. Unless you're very experienced at knotting, don't tackle an advanced project until you've tried out a few of the easier ones.

THE ROUGH SKETCH

As with any art project, preparation is vital. It saves time, helps you prevent mistakes, and ensures your necklace will fit you. That doesn't mean you can't change things as you proceed with the knotting—I almost always change *something*—but a well-thought-out sketch helps you keep a picture in your mind of the effect you are trying to achieve. I find that a sketch is essential, whether you're working with my projects or on your own. It doesn't have to be perfect; it acts as a rough guide. Tape it right to your macramé board and work over it.

Consider these three questions when making your rough sketch:

1. Am I making this jewelry for me or someone else? Do I need jewelry to go with a particular outfit?

2. Do I have some special beads/fiber that I want to work with?

3. What style, length, and size necklace or other piece do I wish to make?

If you are going to make a piece of jewelry for someone else, pick what you think they might like. If you want a piece of jewelry for yourself, to go with a specific outfit, then your color range is limited to those colors. Pick out beads and fibers that are possibilities.

If you have some special items you want to work with, gather them up, along with any other beads or fibers that could possibly work with them. Rearrange them on a tray. Try pairing different items together to see which matches work well and which do not.

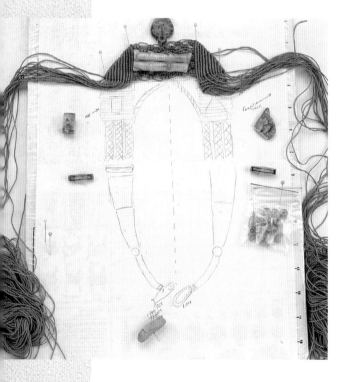

If you are designing for yourself or a certain person, decide if you want a short necklace that fits right around the base of the neck or a longer piece that falls below the clothing neckline. It may help to take a piece of cord, thread on the focal bead, and hold it up to your neck while looking in a mirror. When you find the right length, divide it in half and draw a line down your paper as a guide.

In the case of a fitted necklace—such as the Lacy Collar Necklace on page 55—you can cut out the shape of the necklace, place it around your neck, and then alter it to fit.

Jane Olson-Phillips
Ancient Fish, 2007
29 inches (73.6 cm)
Natural linen and green cotton cord, carved stone fish, stone disk, clay fish toggle, wood
Photo by Stewart O'Shields

Kris Buchanan
Green & Turquoise Freeform Macrame Necklace, 2007
12 x 2 x ½ inches (30.5 x 5.1 x 1.3 cm)
Cord, beads, tantrum
Tantrum by JoElla Johnson
Photo by artist

GETTING STARTED

BALANCING YOUR JEWELRY

When creating jewelry, try to achieve a balance of space and weight. Keep the heavier or larger beads close to the focal bead. If the beads on one side of a necklace are heavier than those on the other, the necklace won't settle nicely. A necklace can be symmetrical or asymmetrical, but it must be in balance.

See the Southwest Picot Choker (page 38) and Double Donuts (page 68) projects for examples of symmetrical arrangement. See the Iridescent Bubbles (page 25), Black & White Necklace (page 44), and Stones, Bones & Fossils (page 88) projects for asymmetric examples. For the last one, I had to carefully work out the size, weight, and balance of all the components in order to create a necklace that hung correctly.

USING THE ROUGH SKETCH

When creating a rough sketch for a piece such as a necklace, you should start by drawing the fastenings on your sketch. Then, holding your board flat, lay out (or pin) pony beads (page 20) at least 2 inches (5 cm) from the fastening. The 2-inch space is not usually seen, so don't waste beads there. Instead, you'll use the space for knotting. Draw your focal bead or pendant on the paper next. The space left is your designing area.

Decide on the width—will it be one large knotted strand like the Spiral Choker (page 22) or do you want a wider combination of beads and knots? Mark off where your beads will lie as a guide for the knotting you'll do.

When you design your own piece, think about what knots you would like to use and where the beads will fit in. Look to the project photos in the book for ideas of how a certain area of knotting will look. Mark or write it onto your sketch. You can always change it if it doesn't work.

BEGINNING A NECKLACE

Here are some ways you can work a necklace from the beginning:

1 Start at the back of the necklace by threading cords through the loop on the fastening. Pin the fastening to the top of your board and work down to the focal point or center. Turn the board and work toward the back, carefully lining up the knotting with the side already finished. Finish off by attaching to a ring or toggle bar, or by making a loop (page 20).

2 If all your cords will not fit through the loop on the fastening, add a split ring or jump ring that will hold all the cords. Alternatively, thread all the cords you can through the loop on the fastening. Find the center of the cords that wouldn't fit through and place it over the fastening, leaving cords hanging below and stretched out above. Take a left-hand cord and a right-hand cord from the cords going through the loop and tie a Square Knot (SK) over the looped cords and the extra ones on

top. Pull down the cords above and tie a SK over all cords. All your cords are now enclosed in a SK. More SKs will hold them securely.

3 Start the necklace at the center of the focal point. Pin the bead or pendant at the top of your board and knot down each side to the back. See the Black & White Necklace (page 44), Double Donuts (page 68), Funky Ceramic Bead Necklace (page 40), and Stones, Bones & Fossils (page 88) projects.

4 Knot a necklace that slips over your head. Find the center of your cut cords, and then tape and pin them to the top of your board. Work from back to front on both sides, ending with a bead and knot or a whipped binding. See the Muted Multicolored Necklace (page 46) and Primary Colors Necklace (page 100) projects.

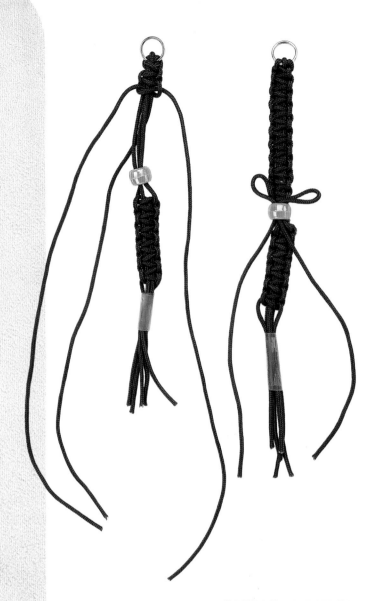

1 When approaching the end of your necklace, stop before you thread on the pony bead. To finish, you will need the two knotting cords you just used and two filler cords. If your cords are too short for the finish, add in a new doubled cord before reaching this spot.

2 Carefully cut out the remaining filler cords. If you are worried about the ends sticking out, place a small dab of glue on them and let them dry.

3 Thread on the pony bead and then thread the cords through the loop or ring of the fastening.

4 Pin the fastening in position on the board opposite the other end of the necklace. Let the cord ends hang down over the cords between the pony bead and the fastening.

5 With an outer left-hand and right hand cord, tie square knots (SK) over all cords at the fastening end. Then SK back to the pony bead. Cut off any hanging filler cord ends.

6 Tie a tight SK with the knotting cords. There should be no fillers.

7 Thread the two cord ends onto a needle or wire and pull the knot into the pony bead. Place a drop of glue where you pulled the knot into the bead.

8 Then pull in and cut off the ends on the other side of the bead.

FINISHING A NECKLACE

I finished all of my necklaces with hidden ends, a tassel or fringe. I don't like to have ends and knots showing. If you need a small ring on the end of your necklace, try to use a split ring instead of a jump ring, as they are much stronger.

I also use "pony beads" a lot. These beads—whether glass, plastic, or metal—are very useful for hiding cords and knots. They have large holes (4 mm or about ⅛ inch), but are fairly small beads (5 to 6 mm or about ¼ inch). You don't have to use them; just find another large-holed bead that matches the other beads in your necklace.

MAKING A LOOP

When working with fiber, a loop just seems to blend in and become a part of the necklace. The toggle can be a bead, button, stick, or a shape like a bird or fish that you have made from polymer clay. You can paint them or even have your name on them, but they should fit in with the rest of the necklace.

1 After threading on your pony bead, extend your cords straight over the top end of the board.

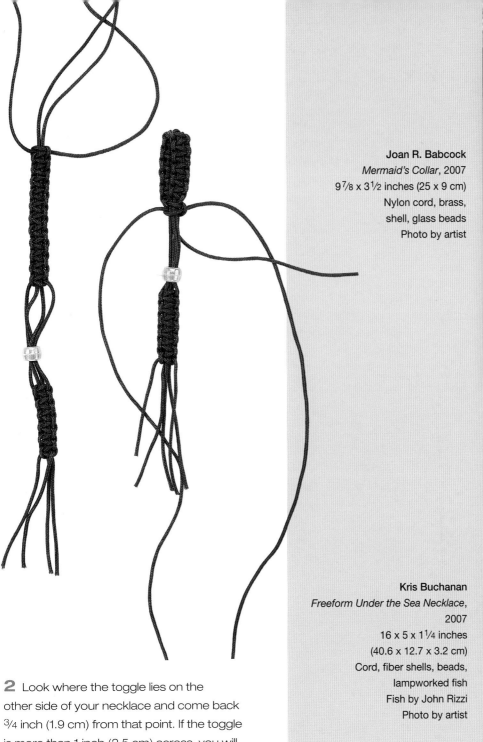

Joan R. Babcock
Mermaid's Collar, 2007
9⁷⁄₈ x 3¹⁄₂ inches (25 x 9 cm)
Nylon cord, brass,
shell, glass beads
Photo by artist

Kris Buchanan
Freeform Under the Sea Necklace,
2007
16 x 5 x 1¹⁄₄ inches
(40.6 x 12.7 x 3.2 cm)
Cord, fiber shells, beads,
lampworked fish
Fish by John Rizzi
Photo by artist

2 Look where the toggle lies on the other side of your necklace and come back ³⁄₄ inch (1.9 cm) from that point. If the toggle is more than 1 inch (2.5 cm) across, you will have to come back further.

3 Turn the board around and SK from that point for 1 inch (2.5 cm). Bend the knotting over and check to see if the toggle piece will fit through the loop.

4 Pin the loop down, turn the board back around, and SK over all cords back to the pony bead. Finish as described above.

SPIRAL CHOKER

EASY

ENAMELED BEAD BY BARBARA MINOR

These simple projects (the choker and a bracelet variation) use only two knots. They're perfect for practicing your knotting skills while showcasing one or more special beads.

WHAT YOU DO

1 Create a half-size sketch of your choker to attach to your knotting board. It will show you where to add your beads as you knot. Draw a 9-inch (22.9 cm) line down the center of your paper. Mark off a 2-inch (5.1 cm) length before the first pony bead. The rest of the line will guide your knotting until you add the focal bead.

2 Thread all four cords through the loop on the claw clasp, doubling the cords. Pin the clasp to the board. With the two outer cords, SK over all the cords for 2 inches (5.1 cm). Thread on the pony bead.

3 Using the two outer cords, HK over the center cords until you reach the 9-inch (22.9 cm) point on your drawing. Thread on your focal bead as desired (page 121). Secure it with pins. Then reverse the board and knot back down the other side.

4 Continue knotting until you reach the point for the other pony bead. Cut out three or four of the shortest cords, put on the pony bead, and continue per the ending instructions (page 20).

5 Thread on the second half of the clasp. Pin in place on your board. Make sure you have at least two cords 20 inches (50.8 cm) long. Double the cords.

6 With a left-hand cord and a right-hand cord, SK over all the cords back toward the pony bead. Cut off the ends of the other cords (not the knotting cords).

7 Tie a SK with the knotting cords. Using a needle or wire, pull the ends of the cords through the pony bead. Place a small amount of white glue on the cords where you pulled them into the bead. Cut off the ends.

FINISHED LENGTH
18 inches (45.7 cm)

WHAT YOU NEED
Macramé board and knotting tools (page 14)

4 linen or hemp cords, each 3$\frac{1}{2}$ yards (3.2 m) in length

Lobster claw clasp, split ring

2 pony beads

Focal bead

KNOTS USED
HK—Half Knot (page 113)

SK—Square Knot (page 114)

TIP

You can run the cords through the focal bead (if they fit), or you can use a wire loop to hang the bead as a pendant.

BRACELET VARIATION

EASY

FINISHED LENGTH

7¼ inches (18.4 cm)

WHAT YOU NEED

Macramé board and knotting tools
(page 14)

4 linen or hemp cords, each 1¾ yards
(1.6 m) in length

Bolt ring clasp

2 pony beads

6 small ⅜-inch (1 cm) beads

½-inch (medium-sized) focal bead

KNOTS USED

HK—Half Knot (page 113)

SK—Square Knot (page 114)

WHAT YOU DO

1 Draw the whole length on the paper. Mark the placement of your beads on the paper.

2 Follow the directions for the choker, beginning with step 2 (page 23).

TIP

Exchange the outside knotting cords after knotting a few inches (5 to 6 cm) to prevent running out of cord.

IRIDESCENT BUBBLES

EASY

This airy necklace highlights large blown-glass beads and multicolored cotton and rayon cord. A button toggle and loop keep it from floating away.

WHAT YOU DO

1 If you're using a large bead for the pendant, put it on the wire with a smaller bead on the top and bottom, if desired. Make a loop with the wire on the top. On the bottom, coil up the wire until reaching the bead. Center the wire under the large bead.

2 Draw a 12-inch (30.5 cm) line on your board from top to bottom. Pin the toggle or button on top of the line.

3 Since the cords probably will not all fit through the toggle or button, you'll need to add some cords (see page 119). Pull one cord through the toggle and center it. Place the three remaining cords over this one. Using the outermost cord on the left and right sides, knot a HK. Pull down the cords above (to add them) and complete a HK as a SK. Continue SKs over all the cords for 3 inches (7.6 cm).

4 Put on one of the large-holed beads over all the cords and pull it over the last knot. If this doesn't hold it in place, tie an OHK first and then pull it inside the bead. Make three SKs.

FINISHED LENGTH
24 inches (61 cm)

WHAT YOU NEED
Macramé board and knotting tools (page 14)

Large focal bead or pendant

#18 wire, 6 inches (15.2 cm) long (if using the large bead as the pendant)

Button or metal toggle

4 cords, each 3 yards (2.7 m) in length

12 matching beads of various sizes with holes large enough for cords

2 matching 13-mm to 19-mm beads with extra-large holes

KNOTS USED
HK—Half Knot (page 113)

SK—Square Knot (page 114)

OHK—Overhand Knot (page 113)

5 On the paper line, mark off the middle of the space remaining to reach the focal bead. Then draw where you want to put the two large beads and the twelve smaller beads. Begin putting on the beads. Tie an OHK under each to hold it in place. At the marked middle spot, knot three SKs and then put on three more beads. If desired, put on extra OHKs in the cords that do not have a bead.

6 When you reach the center, make five HKs. Thread on the focal bead or pendant and do five more HKs. Reverse the board and pins. Continue knotting to the three SKs, placing on small and large beads where needed, and on to the last bead.

7 Leaving the two outer cords, place glue for ¼ inch (6 mm) on the center cords. Let it dry, and then put on the second large-holed bead. Cut off all the cords except for a center cord and two outer cords.

8 Make a loop for the toggle by beginning to knot 2 inches (5.1 cm) from the bead. (See the instructions for "Making a Loop" on page 20.) SK 1½ inches (3.8 cm) for the loop. Knot over all the cords back to the bead, toward the ends. Cut off the center cord. Tie a knot in the two remaining cords and pull the ends and the knot through the bead, placing some glue on the part that will remain in the bead. Trim the ends.

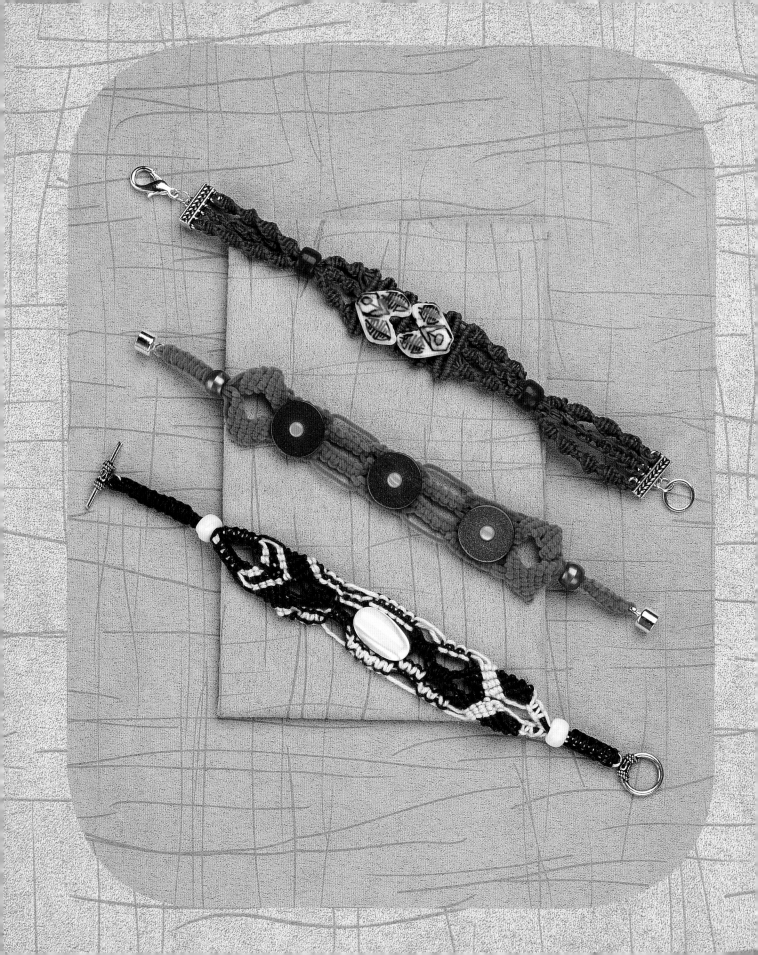

A TRIO OF BRACELETS

Bracelets are always fun to make and wear. To make sure one fits properly, you must draw its design on your board. Knotting and pinning right over your drawing guarantees a bracelet that feels as good as it looks.

BLACK & PEARL BRACELET
This bracelet displays a nugget of mother-of-pearl. Mixing the two colors of the knotting cord demonstrates how the color effect can move within the knotted piece.

WHAT YOU DO

1 Thread all the cords through the fastening to center and double up. Take one outside black cord from each side and tie seven SKs over all cords. Thread on the first small pearl bead.

2 Divide the cords into two groups with four black cords and two white cords in each group. Using the two white cords of the left-hand group as knotting cords, tie two SKs over the four black cords and pin them down. Repeat with the other group.

3 In the left-hand group, line up the cords as follows: one white, four black, and one white. HCH each of the other cords over the left-hand cord (as a filler cord), slanting the knotting down toward the center. Picking up the next cord on the left as a new filler cord, HCH over it and knot in the filler cord from the first row. Repeat knotting over the filler cords from the left until you have knotted seven rows. Repeat the process with the group on the right, using the right-hand cord as a filler cord, knotting and slanting toward the center.

4 Of the four center cords, use the left- and right-hand outer cords to tie three SKs over the two center cords.

5 Leaving two cords out on each side, line up two white cords and two black cords on the left side, and tie three SKs. On the right side, line up two black cords and two white cords, and tie three more SKs.

6 Thread the pearl nugget on the two center cords and pull it out of the way. Of the five cords on the left, use the left- and right-hand cords as knotting cords and tie five SKs over the three filler cords. Repeat with the five cords on the right.

7 Pull down the nugget and cords. Leaving two cords off on each side, divide the rest of the cords into two groups of four. In the left-hand group, use the outside left- and outside right-hand cords to tie three SKs over the two filler cords. Repeat on the right side.

FINISHED LENGTH
8 inches (20.3 cm)

WHAT YOU NEED
4 black linen cords, each 1$\frac{1}{2}$ yards (1.4 m) in length

2 white linen cords, each 1$\frac{1}{2}$ yards (1.4 m) in length

2 small pearl beads with large holes

Pearl nugget, $\frac{3}{4}$ inch long, with hole

Silver toggle

KNOTS USED
SK—Square Knot (page 114)

HCH—Horizontal Clove Hitch (page 115)

8 Divide the cords into three groups of four and tie three SKs with each group. Divide the cords into two groups of six cords, lining up the colors as you like. With the left-hand cord as a filler, HCH each of the five cords in turn. Repeat on the right side as you did in step 3.

9 Divide the cords into two even groups and use the left- and right-hand cords to tie three SKs over the filler cords. Repeat on the right side. Trim off three of the filler cords in each group. Place a dab of glue on the ends and let them dry.

10 With the outside left- and right-hand cords, tie a SK over all the cords. Thread on the second small pearl bead. Pull the cords through the loop on the fastening and finish as usual.

BUTTONED ORANGE BRACELET
This bracelet has a pattern of lines and circles. Three bright turquoise buttons contrast beautifully against the orange suede cord. A magnetic clasp makes it easy to put on and take off.

WHAT YOU DO

1 Thread the cords through the loop in the clasp to the center point and double them up. Use an outside cord from each side as knotting cords to tie seven SKs over all the filler cords. Thread on the first pony bead.

2 Divide the cords into two groups of five. Use the right-hand cord of the left-hand group as a filler cord and HCH each of the four cords over it toward the left. Repeat, using the next outside cord on the right. Be sure to knot the previous filler cord each time. Continue for three rows.

3 Use the left-hand cord of the right-hand group as a filler cord. Tie three rows of HCHs, knotting from left to right.

FINISHED LENGTH
7$\frac{1}{2}$ inches (19 cm)

WHAT YOU NEED
5 cords of suede yarn, each 1$\frac{1}{2}$ yards (1.4 m) in length

Magnetic clasp

2 pony beads

3 buttons, $\frac{3}{4}$-inch (1.9 cm) in diameter

KNOTS USED
SK—Square Knot (page 114)

HCH—Horizontal Clove Hitch (page 115)

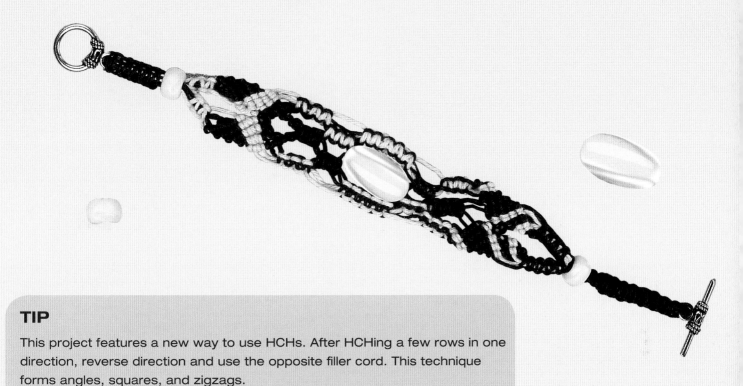

TIP

This project features a new way to use HCHs. After HCHing a few rows in one direction, reverse direction and use the opposite filler cord. This technique forms angles, squares, and zigzags.

4 Knot in the opposite direction with the left-hand group. Use the left-hand cord as a filler cord and knot from left to right. Repeat for three rows. Knot in the opposite direction with the right-hand group. Use the right-hand cord as a filler cord and knot from right to left.

5 Use the outside left and right cords of the four center cords to tie two SKs over the other two cords. Thread the two filler cords through the loop on the first button. Repeat the two SKs.

6 With the three cords on the left side, tie five SKs over one filler cord. Repeat on the right side.

7 Leave out one cord on each side. Use the outside cords from the four cords on the left to tie five SKs over two filler cords. Repeat on the right side. Be sure to pin down the knotting.

8 Bring down the cords on the left and right. Tie six SKs with the left and right cords from the three cords on the left (with one as a filler cord). Repeat with the three cords on the right. Use the four center cords to repeat step 5, tying three SKs before and after adding each button.

9 Repeat steps 6 to 8.

10 Repeat steps 2 to 4.

11 Use the outside cords on the left and right to tie two SKs over the eight remaining cords. Cut out four of the filler cords. Place a dab of glue on the cut ends and allow them to dry. Thread on the second pony bead.

12 Thread the remaining cords through the loop on the fastening. Turn the bracelet around and pin the fastening in place. With the outside left- and right-hand cords, SK over the filler cords back to the pony bead. Cut off the filler cords and finish as usual.

BLUE BRACELET WITH PORCELAIN BEADS

This multi-strand bracelet uses a three-strand separator bar to hold the cords. The two flat Chinese porcelain beads form a raised diamond pattern.

WHAT YOU DO

1 Connect the first jump ring to the separator bar and the lobster clasp. Connect the other jump ring to the 5/8-inch (1.6 cm) ring and the separator bar. Draw a line on the paper on your board the exact length of the bracelet and pin on the fastenings. Measure the distance between the fastenings and also mark the halfway point. This is your knotting distance. Sketch in your beads (page 16).

2 Thread three cords through the left-hand loop of the separator bar. Double them up and use a left- and right-hand cord to HK over the four filler cords for 1 1/2 inches (3.8 cm). Repeat with the three cords doubled on the right-hand side. Using two cords at a time from the four center cords, alternately HH around the other two cords for 1 1/2 inches (3.8 cm).

3 Thread on one of the pony beads and continue to HK for 3/4 inch (1.9 cm) as above. Pin the knotting to your board. Tape the four center cords to the top of the board. Use the two right-hand cords as filler cords and HCH each cord over them. Continue HCHs back and forth for ten rows, leaving a slight space between each row.

4 From the four center cords, use the wire needle to pull two cords under the first row of knotting and up through. Thread the four cords through one of the large beads, pulling the cords down and under a row and then up. Thread on the second large bead, again pulling two of the cords under and up.

5 Divide the cords into three groups: one with six, one with four, and one with six. HH the two groups on each side group for 3/4 inch (1.9 cm) as above. Cut out three cords from the six-cord group and one cord from the center group. Thread the cords through the loops in the separator bars the same as in step 2 and finish off. The center group can be HHed around the filler cord.

THREE SQUARES
Necklace

INTERMEDIATE

I chose three pretty, natural stone squares here, but you could also use stone circles or donuts. This piece combines howlite squares with a vintage black button for a toggle, black and white bone beads, a mixture of small black and white beads, and a black cord.

WHAT YOU DO

1 Pick out your center square stone. One at a time, find the center of five cords and LHK them onto one side of the stone. Pull tight. Using an outside left-hand cord and an outside right-hand cord, SK for three knots over all the cords.

2 Divide the cords into a top and bottom layer. Run the bottom layer (five cords) up through the second stone from underneath. Bring the top cords over and, with a left-hand and a right-hand cord, tie five SKs over all the cords.

3 Divide the cords again into top and bottom layers. Bring them under and over (respectively) the other side of the second stone square. Using a left- and right-hand cord, knot four SKs over all the cords. Thread on one of the large beads.

TIP

When stringing the matching beads, balance the sizes and colors on the necklace. If any beads have very small holes (too small for threading cords), you can sew them on afterward.

FINISHED LENGTH
22 inches (55.9 cm)

WHAT YOU NEED
Macramé board and knotting tools (page 14)

3 square stones, about 1 3/4 inch (4.4 cm) square

10 cords, each 2 yards (1.8 m) in length

1 cord, 1 1/2 yards (1.4 m) in length

4 10-mm large beads with large holes

2 pony beads

Clasp fastening

Medium tapestry needle

An assortment of matching beads, size #6 and up

KNOTS USED
SK—Square Knot (page 114)

HK—Half Knot (page 113)

LHK—Lark's Head Knot (page 112)

OHK—Overhand Knot (page 113)

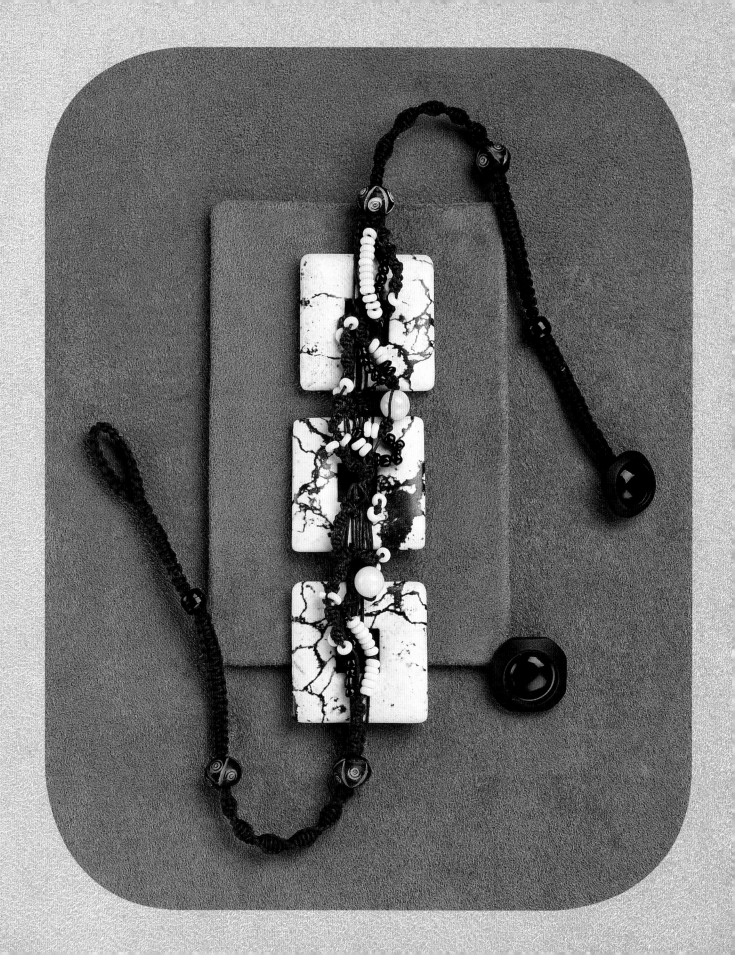

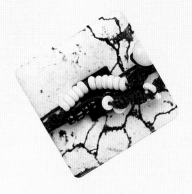

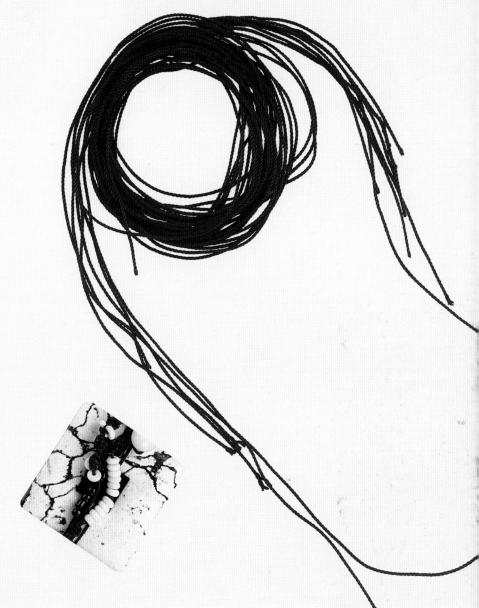

4 Repeat steps 1 to 3 on the other side of the middle square. Keep the stones and knotting pinned in place.

5 Starting on the right side of the necklace, tie a HK with a left and right cord over all the cords for 2 inches (5.1 cm). Thread on another large bead and repeat the HK for 2 more inches (5.1 cm).

6 Cut out six cords from the center of the filler cords. Put on one of the pony beads and thread the remaining cords through the fastening. SK over all the cords for 2 inches (5.1 cm) back toward the necklace. Finish as described on page 20. Repeat on the other side.

7 Put the 1½-yard (1.4 m) cord on the medium tapestry needle and pull the cord through the knotting, just under the large bead. Double up the cord and put glue on the ends. Let it dry, shaping the ends sharp enough to pull through the beads.

8 Put nine #6 beads on one cord and pull it under the knotting in the center of the square. Tie an OHK in the cord to keep the beads in place. Continue adding beads in and out of the knotting and squares, tying a knot every 1 inch (2.5 cm) or 1½ inch (3.8 cm), until you reach the other side of the squares. Pull the end out of sight and tie an OHK around the cord.

9 Repeat step 8 with the remaining half of the doubled cord. You can't go wrong with the "ins and outs" as long as you distribute the beads over the squares in a balanced way.

STYLISHLY HEMP
Necklace

EASY

This project teaches you how to combine the square knot and half knot to produce a fuller look. Instead of using just four cords doubled, this design adds another single cord, allowing you to knot three sets of multiple strands. I used natural linen to complement the focal bead, but you can also use hemp, cotton, or stiff rayon.

WHAT YOU DO

1 Thread the four 3½-yard (3.2 m) cords through the loop on the clasp, doubling the cords. Pin the clasp to your board. Lay the 1½-yard (1.4 m) cord over the other cords, leaving a 3-inch (7.6 cm) tail above the clasp.

2 Using an outer left cord and outer right cord, tie a HK over all the cords. Bring the tail down and finish making a SK. Continue SKs for 2 inches (5.1 cm), knotting in the tail with the other cords. Cut the excess from the tail. Thread the cords through one of the pony beads.

3 Divide the cords into two groups, one with four cords and the other with five. With a right and a left outer cord of one group, HK for 2 inches (5.1 cm). Repeat with the other group. Twist the two groups together.

4 Knot one SK over all the cords with an outer left and an outer right cord. Thread the two small beads on these outer cords. Continue knotting SKs over all the other cords for 1½ inches (3.8 cm).

5 Thread on the first cylindrical bead. If all the cords will not fit through the bead hole,

pull a center cord through the bead and run the other cords outside the bead. Knot one SK with the right- and left-hand cords over all the cords.

6 Divide the cords into three groups of three cords for a multi-strand section. Using the left- and right-hand cords of one group, knot HKs over the filler cord for 2 inches (5.1 cm). Repeat this step with the other two groups, choosing the longer cords as the knotting cords.

7 Bring the three groups together and thread on one of the 13-mm beads. HK the left-hand cord and the right-hand cord for ½ inch (1.3 cm) over all the cords. Thread on the focal bead.

8 Pin the focal bead in place, reverse the board, and continue knotting the other side. Make sure to line up the knotting with the first side. When you have reached the space for the pony bead, cut out four cords—do not cut the knotting cords; just cut the shortest of the remaining cords. Thread the remaining cords through the split ring and finish as outlined on page 20.

FINISHED LENGTH
20 inches (50.8 cm)

WHAT YOU NEED
Macramé board and knotting tools (page 14)

4 cords, each 3½ yards (3.2 m) in length

1 cord, 1½ yards (1.4 m) in length

Lobster clasp, split ring

2 pony beads

2 smaller beads

2 cylindrical beads

2 13-mm beads

Large focal bead

KNOTS USED
HK—Half Knot (page 113)

SK—Square Knot (page 114)

SOUTHWEST PICOT
Choker

EASY

The alternating half-hitch knot gives this choker a swirly pattern, while the picot knots add a lacy touch. You'll love watching the effect appear as you work.

WHAT YOU DO

1 Use four cords for each side of the donut bead. Double the cords and secure them one at a time to the donut with a LHK. Pin the donut bead to your work board. Using a left-hand cord and a right-hand cord, SK for 1 inch (2.5 cm) and then thread on one of the 10-mm beads. If all the cords will not fit through the bead, thread one and run the others behind the bead.

2 Using an outer left- and outer right-hand cord, tie one SK over all the filler cords. Then tie five SKPs. Finish with one SK.

3 Thread a middle cord through one of the animal beads—usually only one cord will fit through the bead hole, so run the others along the back. Tie one SK using the left- and right-hand cords over all the filler cords.

4 Divide the cords into two groups of four cords each. Using the left-hand and right-hand cords, HK for 1¾ inches (4.4 cm) over the filler cord. Repeat with the other four cords. Thread on one of the 8-mm beads.

5 Keep four cords in the center as filler cords and pull two cords out to each side. Tie AHHs. Loop the two cords on the left over the filler cords and up underneath. Loop the right-hand cords over the filler cords and back underneath. Repeat for 1½ inches (3.8 cm). Tie one SK with the outside cords over all the filler cords. Cut out the four shortest filler cords. Thread on the last pony bead, and then thread the cords through the toggle loop. Finish with SKs back to the pony bead as described on page 20.

6 Repeat on the other side. Finish by following the instructions in the section "Making a Loop" on page 20.

FINISHED LENGTH
18 inches (45.7 cm)

WHAT YOU NEED
Macramé board and knotting tools (page 14)

8 cords of black linen, each 3 yards (2.7 m) in length

Stone or glass donut bead, 1 inch (2.5 cm) in diameter

2 10-mm beads

2 carved animal beads

2 8-mm beads with large holes

2 pony beads

Toggle or button

KNOTS USED
HK—Half Knot (page 113)

LHK—Lark's Head Knot (page 112)

SK—Square Knot (page 114)

AHH—Alternating Half Hitch (page 114)

Special Knot SKP—Square Knot Picot

To tie a SKP, tie the first half of a SK. Start the second half of the SK about ½ inch (1.3 cm) below the first half. Push the second half up to the first to complete the SK and form the picot loop.

FUNKY CERAMIC BEAD
Necklace

INTERMEDIATE

BEADS BY JENNIFER HEYNEN

Matching the cords to the beads continues the theme of chartreuse, black-and-white swirls, dots, and lines. Mixing the colors in the knotting helps bring the whole package together.

WHAT YOU DO

1 Thread one piece of the black tape yarn, black cord, and chartreuse cord through the left loop of the pendant and double up the cords. (Use the left loop, as you look at the pendant pinned on upside down.) Using the chartreuse cords as knotting cords, SK for 1½ inches (3.8 cm) over the remaining cords. Do not tie the knots close together—the black yarns can show through. Tie a SK without filler cords with the two chartreuse cords.

2 Thread one black cord and one chartreuse cord through the cylinder bead. To hold the large bead in place, tie one SK without filler cords using the threaded two cords and the remaining black and chartreuse cords.

3 SK over the other cords for 1¼ inches (3.2 cm) with the chartreuse cord from the left side and the black cord from the right side. Run the black tape yarn behind the large round or triangular bead. Then thread the other cords through the bead.

4 Divide the cords into two even groups. HK over one of the black tape yarn pieces for 1½ inches (3.8 cm) using the two black cords as knotting cords. Repeat over the other black tape yarn piece with the two chartreuse cords. Thread the chartreuse and black cords through the first small triangle bead. Run the black tape yarn along the back. Bringing all the cords together, use the black cords as knotting cords to SK for 2 inches (5.1 cm) over all the cords. Carefully cut out the black tape yarn. Thread on the first pony bead.

5 Thread on the toggle and SK back to the pony bead over all the cords. Finish as usual.

6 Repeat steps 1 to 5 to complete the other side of necklace, finishing off with a loop for the toggle.

7 For a fun touch, cut six pieces of the black tape yarn, each 6 inches (15.2 cm) long. Tie these pieces through the loops of the pendant, above and behind the cylinder beads, the round bead, and the triangle bead. Tie an SK and allow the ends to hang down like fringe. Put a dab of glue on the ends to prevent fraying.

FINISHED LENGTH

24 inches (61 cm)

WHAT YOU NEED

2 pieces of black polyamide knitting tape yarn, each 2 yards (1.8 m) in length

2 black rayon cords, each 3 yards (2.7 m) in length

2 chartreuse embroidery cotton cords, each 2½ yards (2.3 m) in length

Ceramic pendant bead, 2¼ inches (5.7 cm) in diameter

2 2-inch (5.1 cm) curved cylinder ceramic beads

2 1-inch (2.5 cm) ceramic beads (1 circular, 1 triangular)

2 small triangular ceramic beads, ½ inch (1.3 cm) in diameter

2 black pony beads

Toggle

14 black seed beads, size 6

14 chartreuse seed beads, size 6

KNOTS USED

SK—Square Knot (page 114)

HK—Half Knot (page 113)

OHK—Overhand Knot (page 113)

LACY SQUARE KNOT
Choker

EASY

The knots in this choker require a stiff cord such as hemp or linen, and they combine to produce a formal, geometric look. The dichroic pendant adds bright tones that the seed beads pick up and amplify.

WHAT YOU DO

1 Thread the cords through the toggle to the center and double them up. With a left-hand cord and a right-hand cord, tie a SK over all the cords. Continue knotting for 2 inches (5.1 cm). Put on one of the pony beads.

2 Divide the cords into two groups of six cords. Using a left-hand and a right-hand cord from one group, HK over the remaining four cords of that group for ¾ inch (1.9 cm). Repeat with the other group. Pin the two groups to your board. Pin the two left cords in place—they'll act as filler cords. HCH each cord over the filler cord.

3 Begin tying Alternating Square Knots, as follows. Divide the cords into three groups of four cords. In each group, knot three SKs with a left cord and a right cord. For the second row, leave two cords out on each side, and then knot three SKs with each group. Repeat this step (to get four rows of SKs).

4 Pin the last knots down. Using the two right-most cords as fillers, HCH each cord over the fillers, working from right to left. Add five seed beads on alternate cords. Repeat the HCH knots, this time from left to right.

5 Repeat the Alternating Square Knots as in step 3, but begin with the two cords left out on each side, knotting with the two groups.

6 Repeat the HCHs with two filler cords as in step 4, beginning on the left side. Add five beads on alternate cords, and then HCH from the right to the left.

7 Divide the cords into three groups of four cords each. In one group, HK with the left and right cords over the other two cords for 1¼ inch (3.2 cm). Repeat for the other two groups.

8 Thread on the pendant, reverse the board, and pin the knotting and pendant in place. Continue knotting the other side, carefully matching up the knotting with the finished side.

9 Before putting on the last pony bead, carefully cut out the shortest six cords, being sure not to cut the last knotting cords. Put on the pony bead and thread the remaining cords through the bar fastening. Finish as described on page 20.

FINISHED LENGTH
17 inches (43.2 cm)

WHAT YOU NEED
Macramé board and knotting tools (page 14)

6 cords, each 3 yards (2.7 m) in length

Toggle

2 pony beads

20 square seed beads, size 6

Special bead or pendant

KNOTS USED
HK—Half Knot (page 113)

SK—Square Knot (page 114)

HCH—Horizontal Clove Hitch (page 115)

ASK—Alternating Square Knot (see step 3)

TIP
To make this necklace longer or shorter, add or subtract SKs in the first knotting section from the back. Be sure to do it on both sides.

BLACK & WHITE
Necklace

EASY

Black linen, a slice of striped onyx, and Dzi-style glass beads make an elegant combination. You can modify this necklace with any monochrome or two-color focal bead, changing the colors of the fiber to match.

WHAT YOU DO

1 Knot this one from the front to the back (starting in the center). Double three cords in turn. At the loop end, tie a LHK onto the stone. Using one cord from the left side and one from the right, tie a tight HK to hold the cords tightly in place. HK for 1 inch (2.5 cm).

2 Pin the stone in place by placing pins around the edge. Thread two seed beads on a left and a right cord. Tie two more HKs. Thread on the first cylindrical bead. Tie two more HKs, and then add on two more seed beads.

3 Divide the cords into two groups of three cords. With a left-hand and a right-hand cord from one group, HK for 1 inch (2.5 cm). Repeat with the other group. Thread on the next cylindrical bead.

4 Continue to HK with the left- and right-hand cords over all four cords for 1 inch (2.5 cm). Thread on the next cylindrical bead. Repeat the HK for 1 more inch (2.5 cm).

5 Cut out the two shortest cords—but do not cut the last knotting cords—and thread on one of the pony beads. Pull the cords through the clasp. Finish the necklace as described on page 20.

6 Reverse the board and repeat steps 1–5.

TIP
Look for a stone with at least one natural opening or with an uneven edge. Your cords will slip off the stone if they don't have a rough edge to keep them in place. Also, you can vary your arrangement of beads by introducing asymmetry for visual interest.

FINISHED LENGTH
24 inches (61 cm)

WHAT YOU NEED
Macramé board and knotting tools (page 14)

6 cords, each 2 1/2 yards (2.3 m) in length

Stone slice or fragment for the focal piece (see Tip)

8 seed beads or crystals, size 6

4 cylindrical beads, 1 to 1 1/2 inches (2.5 to 3.8 cm) in length

2 round beads, 5/8 inch (1.6 cm) in diameter

2 pony beads

Silver clasp

KNOTS USED
LHK—Lark's Head Knot (page 112)

HK—Half Knot (page 113)

SK—Square Knot (page 114)

OHK—Overhand Knot (page 113)

MUTED MULTICOLOR
Necklace

EASY

I liked this multicolored yarn so much that I made matching polymer clay beads to go with it. The yarn is fairly substantial—it won't droop—but any thick cord will do. The tassel adds interest and movement.

WHAT YOU DO

1 Find the center of all the cords and tape it to your working board. With the outermost left and right cords on one side of the tape, SK for 4 inches (10.2 cm) over all the cords. Pull the cords through the first pony bead.

2 Divide the nine cords into two groups, one with four cords and the other with five. Using the outermost left and right cords of one group, HK for 2½ inches (6.4 cm). Repeat with the other group.

3 Pin the two groups to the board. Using the left cord as the filler cord, HCH each cord in turn over the filler cord. Pull all the cords through one of the smaller beads. Using a right cord as a filler, HCH from right to left.

4 Divide the cords into three groups of three cords each, and knot three SKs on each group. Continue with ASKs. Leaving the outside cords to the side, divide the remaining cords into two groups, one with three cords and the other with four. Knot three ASKs on each. For the next row, divide all the cords back into three groups of three cords each. Knot three more ASKs.

FINISHED LENGTH
30 inches (76.2 cm)

WHAT YOU NEED
Macramé board and knotting tools (page 14)

9 cords, each 4 yards (3.7 m) in length

2 pony beads

2 smaller beads with large holes

2 15-mm medium-sized beads with large holes

25-mm (or larger) bead with a large hole

KNOTS USED
HK—Half Knot (page 113)

SK—Square Knot (page 114)

HCH—Horizontal Clove Hitch (page 115)

VCH—Vertical Clove Hitch (page 117)

OHK—Overhand Knot (page 113)

ASK—Alternating Square Knot (see Lacy Square Knot Choker, step 3, page 43)

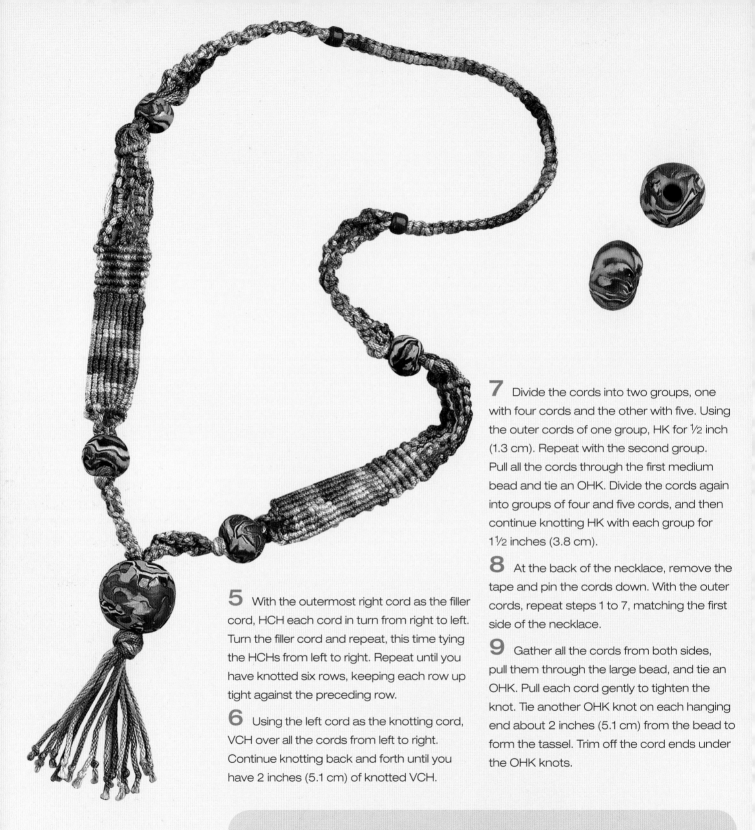

5 With the outermost right cord as the filler cord, HCH each cord in turn from right to left. Turn the filler cord and repeat, this time tying the HCHs from left to right. Repeat until you have knotted six rows, keeping each row up tight against the preceding row.

6 Using the left cord as the knotting cord, VCH over all the cords from left to right. Continue knotting back and forth until you have 2 inches (5.1 cm) of knotted VCH.

7 Divide the cords into two groups, one with four cords and the other with five. Using the outer cords of one group, HK for ½ inch (1.3 cm). Repeat with the second group. Pull all the cords through the first medium bead and tie an OHK. Divide the cords again into groups of four and five cords, and then continue knotting HK with each group for 1½ inches (3.8 cm).

8 At the back of the necklace, remove the tape and pin the cords down. With the outer cords, repeat steps 1 to 7, matching the first side of the necklace.

9 Gather all the cords from both sides, pull them through the large bead, and tie an OHK. Pull each cord gently to tighten the knot. Tie another OHK knot on each hanging end about 2 inches (5.1 cm) from the bead to form the tassel. Trim off the cord ends under the OHK knots.

TIP
You knot this necklace from back to front, ending with a tassel. As you knot, remember to keep switching to the longer cords.

PURPLE POD
Necklace

T his blown-glass pendant reminds me of a seedpod. Purple cotton warp cord emphasizes its color, and the matching crochet cotton and beads complete the effect. I added a matching button as a toggle.

WHAT YOU DO

1 Thread the five long cords through the toggle to the center and double them up. With a left-hand cord and a right-hand cord, SK over all the cords for 2 inches (5.1 cm). Thread on the first pony bead.

2 Divide the cords into two groups of five cords each. Using the left-most cord and right-most cord of one group, HK for 1½ inches (3.8 cm). Repeat with the other group. Twist the two groups together and pin them to your board.

3 HCH over the left-hand cord (as a filler cord) with the remaining nine cords. Using the same filler cord, HCH back to the left side. Repeat these two rows.

4 Divide the cords into two groups of five again. Using a left-hand cord and a right-hand cord of one group, SK for 1 inch (2.5 cm). Thread on one of the 5-mm beads. (If the hole is too large and the bead slips down, tie an OHK under the bead.) SK for another inch (2.5 cm). Repeat with the other group. Pin the knotting down.

5 Repeat step 3, except starting from the right-hand side. Thread the outside cords through a long bead, from each end. Using the left-hand cord as a filler cord, HCH over the nine remaining cords from left to right and back again.

6 Tape down the "tail" of one piece of the embroidery cotton on the left side. Begin VCH with the embroidery cotton. Change colors of thread as desired by dropping one cord and starting another (page 119). Randomly place three seed beads in the knotting—skip the knot when adding the bead. Knot for 1¾ inches (4.4 cm).

FINISHED LENGTH
26 inches (66 cm)

WHAT YOU NEED
5 cords (linen, hemp, cotton, or stiff rayon), each 3½ yards (3.2 m) in length

Matching button toggle

2 pony beads

2 cylindrical beads, each ¾ inch (1.9 cm) in length

4 beads with large holes, each ¼ inch (6 mm) in length

16 seed beads, size 6

2 half-circle beads or drops (optional)

Pendant with a large loop

KNOTS USED
OHK—Overhand Knot (page 113)

SK—Square Knot (page 114)

HK—Half Knot (page 113)

HCH—Horizontal Clove Hitch (page 115)

VCH—Vertical Clove Hitch (page 117)

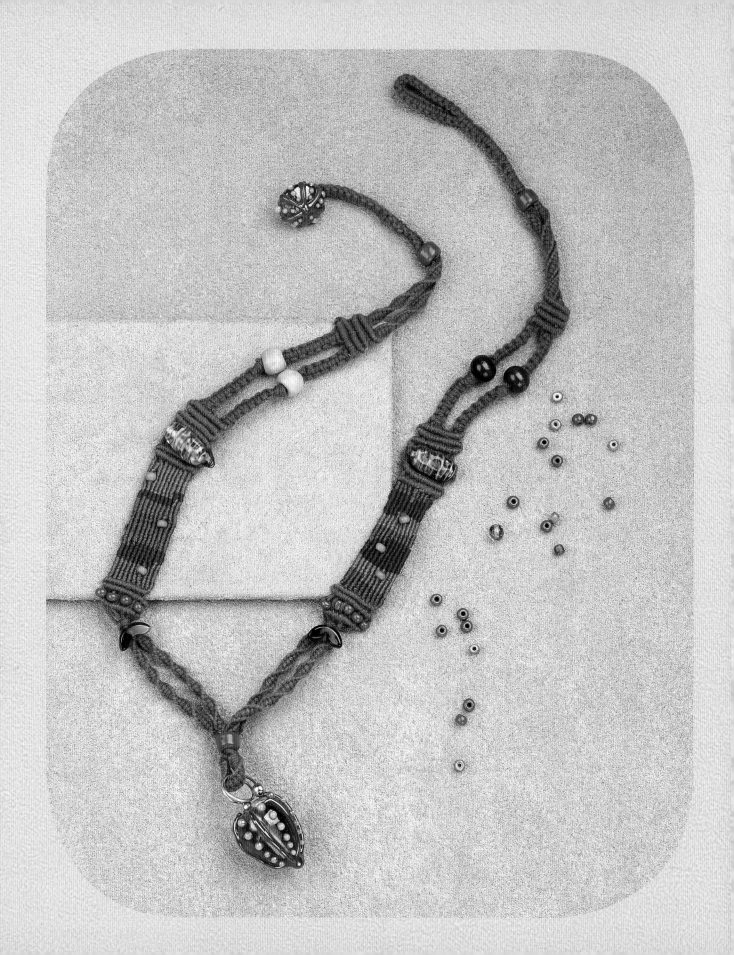

7 With the right-hand cord, HCH to the left and then back to the right. Add on four seed beads on cords #2, #4, #7, and #9 (left to right). Using the right-hand cord as a filler cord, HCH from right to left. With a left-hand cord and a right-hand cord, tie one SK over all the cords. Optionally, thread on the first half-circle bead or drop bead.

8 Divide the cords into two groups of five once more. With the left-most and right-most cords of one group, HK for 2¼ inches (5.7 cm). Put on the second pony bead, and then HK for 1 inch (2.5 cm). Slide on the pendant to the center of the last 1 inch (2.5 cm) of knotting. Pull all the cords through the pony bead and continue HK with the two groups for another 2¼ inches (5.7 cm).

9 Turn your board around and pin down the necklace. Continue as you did on the first side, pinning the work as you go and making sure it matches the first side. When you reach the last pony bead, cut out the four shortest cords, making sure not to cut the knotting cords you just used. Thread on the pony bead and finish with the toggle loop.

KNOT JUST BUTTONS!
Necklace

INTERMEDIATE

Have you ever wondered what to do with those large vintage buttons? I used three different buttons here, all of them the same size and color. Matching seed beads and a button toggle finish off the piece.

WHAT YOU DO

1 Thread six cords through the toggle to the center and double them. (If the cords don't fit through the toggle, see page 121.) Using a left-hand cord and a right-hand cord, SK over the remaining ten cords for 2½ inches (6.4 cm). Thread on the first pony bead.

2 Divide the cords into three groups of four. In one group, using the left-hand and right-hand cords, HK for 1½ inches (3.8 cm). Repeat with the other two groups.

3 Using two cords on the right as filler cords, pin the rest of the cords to your board. HCH over the filler cords from right to left and back again with each cord in turn. Thread four seed beads on alternate cords to create five rows of four seed beads. Repeat two more rows of HCHs from left to right and back.

4 Divide the cords again into three groups of four cords. Using the left- and right-hand cords of one group, tie two SKs. Repeat for the other two groups. Leaving two cords out on each side, tie two SKs on each side. Repeat alternating these knots (Alternating Square Knots, page 43) for five rows.

5 Thread two of the 2-yard (1.8 m) cords onto a large-holed needle or looped wire. Thread these cords behind the cords you knotted in step 4 (cords #3 and #4, left to right). Center the cords. Using a left- and right-hand cord, SK for 2 inches (5.1 cm) over the top of the previous knotting. Repeat with two more cords and thread behind cords #8 and #9 (counting from left to right).

6 Weave these SK cords under and over the ASKs. Let all the cords hang down and pin the knotting cords in place on the board.

FINISHED LENGTH
20 inches (50.8 cm)

WHAT YOU NEED
Macramé board and knotting tools (page 14)

12 cords (linen, hemp, cotton, or stiff rayon) of one color, each 3 yards (2.7 m) in length

8 cords (of any material) of another color, each 2 yards (1.8 m) in length

Toggle button

2 pony beads

60 seed beads, size 6

3 large buttons, at least 1½ inch (3.8 cm) in diameter

Large-holed needle or looped wire

KNOTS USED
SK—Square Knot (page 114)

HK—Half Knot (page 113)

HCH—Horizontal Clove Hitch (page 115)

ASK—Alternating Square Knot (see step 3, page 43)

OHK—Overhand Knot (page 113)

7 You will now tie a series of about ten HCH loops that will curve around to meet the other side of the necklace in the center front. You'll tie the button on the side afterwards. Work with two filler cords and 18 knotting cords.

8 Using the two left-most cords as filler cords, HCH each cord in turn. Leaving a space in the outside curve about ⅜ inches (1 cm) long, taper slightly to the inside edge. Continue knotting back and forth until you have knotted eight outside loops and reached the center.

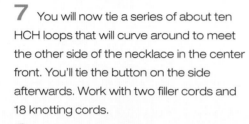

9 Start again on the other side. Find the center of the four cords and tape it down. With an outside left and right cord, SK for 2 to 2½ inches (5.1 to 6.4 cm) to fit around the toggle. Fold up the cord to make a loop and add two more long cords. Continue SKs until you reach the point where you should add the second pony bead. Thread on the bead and pin it on the board opposite the first one. Continue as in steps 2 to 7.

10 Turn the necklace over and bring the sides together. Using three cords from each side on top, tie an OHK. Take the next four cords from each side and tie another OHK. Thread the next two cords from each side through the button shank and tie an OHK. Take the remaining cords and tie an OHK.

11 Allow a 2-inch (5.1 cm) fringe below the button. Place a seed bead on each cord, tie an OHK, and trim. Using two short end pieces of the cord, tie on a side button at around the fourth loop. Repeat with the other button.

TIP
Drawing a sketch of the curve used in step 7 will help guide your knotting.

LACY COLLAR
Necklace

INTERMEDIATE

This is a rounded "collar-like" necklace with accent drops or long beads. You will need to draw a pattern for this on your board. As it fits quite close to the neck, be sure to round off the front section of the necklace for comfort.

WHAT YOU DO

1 Thread six cords through the toggle, center them and double. (If the cords won't fit through the toggle, see page 119.) With a left-hand cord and a right-hand cord, SK over the remaining cords for 2 inches (5.1 cm). Thread on the first pony bead.

2 Divide the cords into two groups of six cords each. Using a left-hand and a right-hand cord from one group, HK for 2 inches (5.1 cm). Repeat with the other group. Twist the two groups together and pin the ends of the knotting to your board.

3 HCH each cord in turn over the left-most cord (as a filler cord). Thread the nuggets on cords #3, #7, and #10, starting from the left.

4 HCH each cord over the right-most cord (as a filler cord). Divide the cords into three groups of four cords.

5 Using the left-hand and right-hand cords in one group, SK over the two filler cords for 2 1/4 inches (5.7 cm). Repeat with the other two groups. Pin down the knotted ends.

6 HCH each cord in turn over the right-most cord (as a filler cord). Add two small disk beads on cords #2, #3, #7, and #8, counting from the left.

7 HCH each cord over the left-most cord (as a filler).

8 Divide the cords again into four groups of three cords. Starting on the left of the first group, tie six AHKs with the left-hand and right-hand cords over two filler cords. Repeat with the other three groups. In the second row, leave one cord out on the left and two on the right. Tie three groups of six AHKs. Repeat with four groups, and then alternate with three groups. Following the pattern, pin the knots down in a curve. On the fifth row, tie two groups of six AHKs on the right side to fill in the space of the curve. Pin the ends of the knotting to the board.

FINISHED LENGTH
22 inches (55.9 cm)

WHAT YOU NEED
6 cords (linen, hemp, or cotton), each 3 1/2 yards (3.2 m) in length

1 cord, 2 yards (1.8 m) in length

Toggle

2 pony beads

6 turquoise nuggets

8 small disks (in a color matching the drops)

5 drops (or any long beads with holes in the end)

4 turquoise disks, 1/2 inch (1.3 cm) in diameter

KNOTS USED
SK—Square Knot (page 114)

HK—Half Knot (page 113)

HCH—Horizontal Clove Hitch (page 115)

AHK—Alternating Half Knot (page 113)

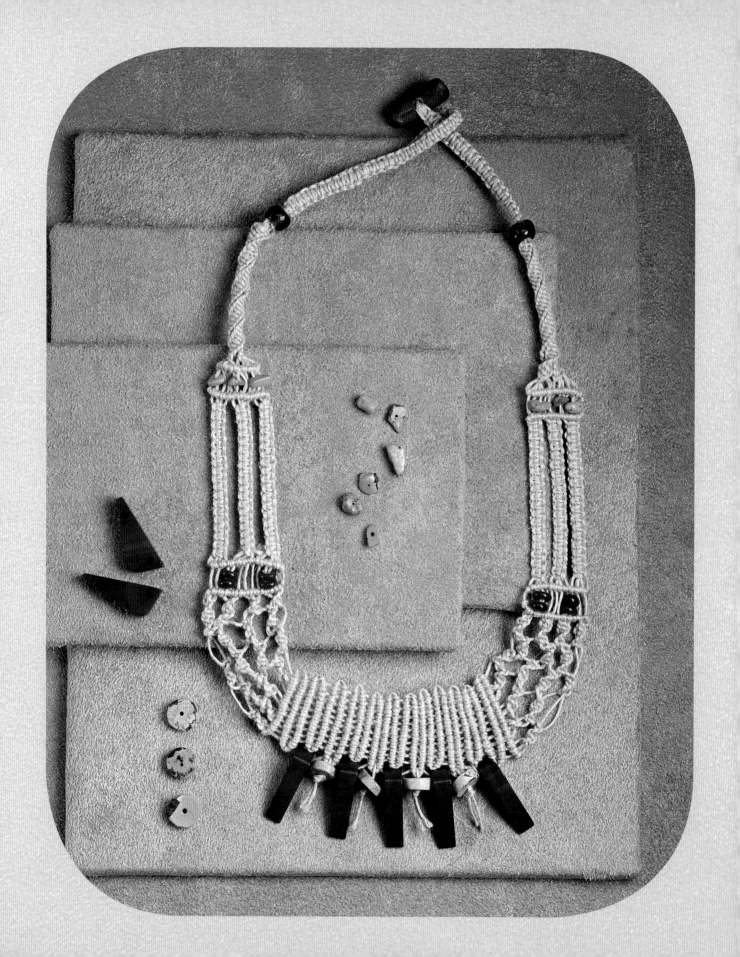

9 Begin HCHs, turning the board as needed. Add the 2-yard (1.8 m) cord as a filler cord on the right side, leaving a 3-inch (7.6 cm) tail taped to the board. Adding a right-hand cord to the new cord, use them both as a filler to add bulk to the knots. HCH all the cords over the filler cords. At the end of each row, add a pin to loop the filler cords around. Knot back to the right side. Continue knotting, leaving out the first knotting cord on the right. Add a drop bead to this cord and leave it loose.

10 HCH the next loop, which is one knot shorter than the previous loop. Knot the cord with the drop bead into the next loop. Continue knotting each row, alternating the longer loop with a drop bead. The longer loops will hold the turquoise disks that you'll add on later. When you're finished with the loops, cut off the shorter filler cord.

11 Divide the cords into four groups of three cords. Using the left- and right-hand cords in the group on the right, HK six knots. Repeat for the next group on the right. This starts the curve in the necklace. Turning the board, leave one cord off on the left side and two cords off on the right side. Divide the cords into three groups of three cords. Using the left- and right-hand cords, HK six knots in each group. Pin the knotting to the board. Continue AHKs for five rows.

12 HCH each cord over the right-hand cord (as a filler cord). Put on the remaining small disks. HCH on the filler cord from left to right.

13 Divide the cords into three groups of four cords. Repeat step 5. Add cords as needed, if any cords become too short.

14 Repeat step 7 using the right-hand cord as a filler.

15 Repeat step 2.

16 Cut out six of the filler cords. Thread on a pony bead and finish with a toggle loop.

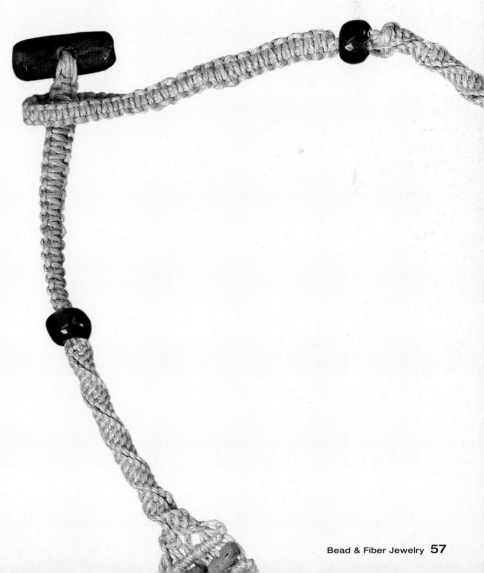

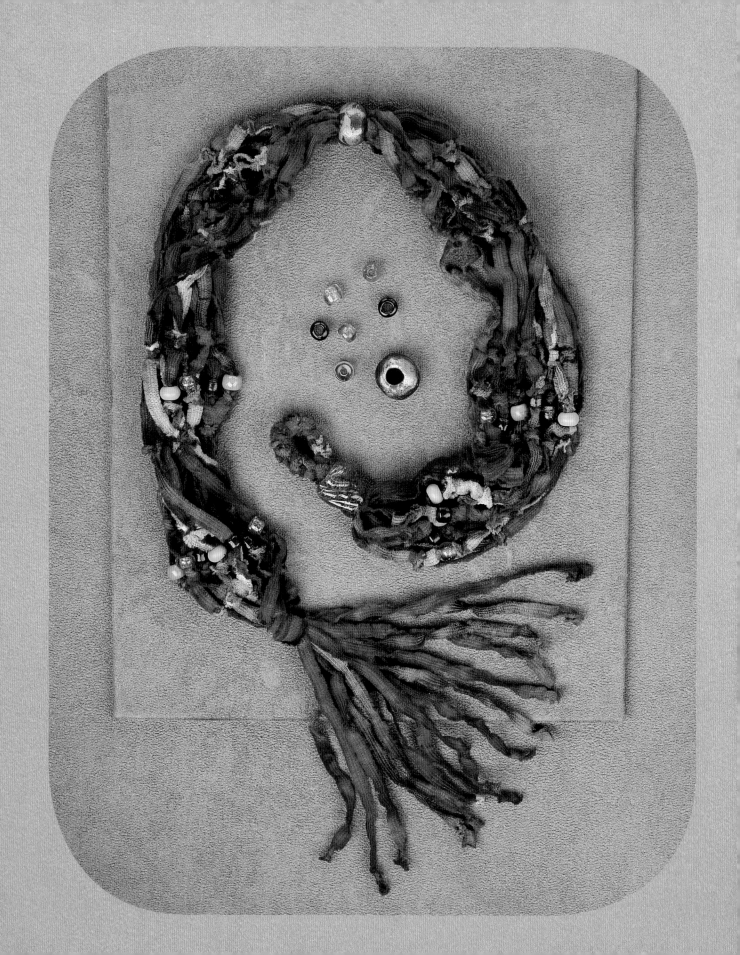

NETTED LARIAT
Necklace
INTERMEDIATE

Use the new multicolored "tape" yarns to make this lariat-type necklace. These yarns come in such a variety, you could make several to go with different outfits. Best of all, this technique is very easy to do—and even if you do make a mistake, no one can tell.

WHAT YOU DO

1 Find the center of the eight cords and tape it to your board. Use a left- and right-hand cord to SK over the other six cords for 2 inches (5.1 cm). Double up the cords to make a loop and pin it to the board. Tie one SK over the 14 cords with a left- and right-hand cord. Thread on the focal bead.

2 After measuring down 1½ inches (3.8 cm) from the bead, tie an OHK with the first two cords on the left. Continue across, tying an OHK with each subsequent two cords. (These are Alternating OHKs.) Leaving a cord out on each side, thread a pony bead on the next two cords. Then tie an OHK with the first two cords on the left, about ½ inch (1.3 cm) down from the last row of knotting. Continue adding pony beads and knotting across the cords. Bring down the outer cords and OHK another row of knots, ½ inch (1.3 cm) down from the second row. Repeat this pattern of three rows of OHKs five more times.

3 Measure 2 inches (5.1 cm) down from the knotting and repeat step 2, adding more pony beads.

4 Measure 2½ inches (6.4 cm) down from the knotting. Leaving out a cord on each side, OHK every two cords as you did in step 2. Knot three rows, leaving out the pony beads.

5 Measure 1½ inches (3.8 cm) down from the knotting and thread on the medium-sized, large-holed bead. This will be the center back.

6 Measure 1½ inches (3.8 cm) down from the medium-sized bead and repeat step 2. Turn the necklace around with the last bead you added in the center back and pin it down.

7 Measure down 1½ inches (3.8 cm) and repeat step 4. Measure down 2½ inches (6.4 cm) and repeat step 2. Measure down another 1½ inches (3.8 cm) and repeat step 2 again.

8 Gather all the cords together and tie an OHK ½ inch (1.3 cm) down from the knotting. Gently pull each cord several times to tighten the knot. Tie an OHK 6 inches (15.2 cm) down on each cord to form a tassel. Trim.

FINISHED LENGTH
29 inches (73.7 cm) to the tassel knot

WHAT YOU NEED
8 cords of multicolored "tape" yarn, each 3½ yards (3.2 m) in length

Focal bead with a hole large enough for the 16 cords

28 pony beads in matching colors

Medium-sized bead with a hole large enough for 16 cords

KNOTS USED
SK—Square Knot (page 114)

OHK—Overhand Knot (page 113)

TIP
The pony beads used here can be any small beads with a hole large enough for one cord.

A QUARTET OF EARRINGS

INTERMEDIATE

Light and airy, fiber earrings are easy on your ears! Find a fiber to match your outfit, add a bead, and choose from these four designs. You're bound to find one to match your style.

BLUE FURNACE GLASS
Matching the cool blue colors of linen cords, rounded glass, and tiny beads makes for striking earrings.

WHAT YOU DO

1 Thread six cords through the first split ring to the center and double them up. Using the outside left- and right-hand cords, tie three SKs and gently pull on the filler cords to make sure they are even in the split ring.

2 Divide the cords into two groups of six cords and tape the right-hand group out of the way. Slanting slightly towards the center, HCH each cord over the left-hand cord (as a filler cord). Start again on the left and HCH each cord in turn, knotting in the hanging filler cord from the first row. Repeat until you have knotted five rows.

3 Repeat the pattern with the other group of cords, starting with the right-hand cord as the filler cord and slanting the knotting toward the center.

4 Pull all the cords together and tie an SK over all the cords, using a left-hand cord from the left side and a right-hand cord from the right side. Thread on the first furnace glass bead and pull the SK into it if possible.

5 Tie an OHK with all the cords. Tighten the knot gently by pulling on each cord individually. Thread the first eight seed beads onto hanging cords, 1 inch (2.5 cm) from the large, furnace glass bead. Tie an OHK under each bead and on the remaining cords. Trim the cords.

6 Repeat to make the other earring. Add the hooks to each split ring.

FINISHED LENGTH
3 to 3 1/2 inches (7.6 to 8.9 cm), not including hooks

WHAT YOU NEED
12 blue linen cords, each 30 inches (76.2 cm) in length

2 6-mm split rings

2 furnace glass beads with 3-mm holes

16 matching seed beads, size 6

2 ear hooks

KNOTS USED
SK—Square Knot (page 114)

HCH—Horizontal Clove Hitch (page 115)

OHK—Overhand Knot (page 113)

TREES IN A FOREST
These lightweight earrings are made from 3-ply linen, sparkly Chinese glass with polka dots, and tiny seed beads.

EASY

WHAT YOU DO

1 Find the center of six of the cords and tape them to your board. Using the outside cords from the left and right sides, tie seven SKs over the four filler cords. Thread on the first split ring to the center of the knotting. Double up the knotting to form a loop and pin it down on the board. Using the outside cords, tie one SK over the ten filler cords.

2 Divide the cords into two groups of six. Using the right-hand cord from the left-hand group as a filler cord, HCH each of the five cords over the filler cord, slanting slightly to the left and down. Repeat with the next right-hand cord, knotting in the filler cord from the first row. Knot four more rows, but do not knot in the previous filler cords.

3 Rest the top filler cord against the knotted rows. HCH over this cord with the remaining filler cord ends.

4 Repeat this pattern with the group of cords on the right side, using the left-hand cord as the filler cord. HCH each of the five cords over the filler cord, slanting slightly to the right and down. Repeat the pattern with the next left-hand cord, knotting in the filler cord from the first row. Knot four more rows, but do not knot in the previous filler cords.

5 Repeat step 3.

6 Divide the cords into three groups of four. Beginning with the group on the left, HK for 1 inch (2.5 cm) with the left- and right-hand cords over the two filler cords. Repeat with the group of cords on the right.

7 Of the four center cords, use the left- and right-hand cords as knotting cords and tie one SK. Thread on the flat disk bead. Tie another SK. Gather all the cords together and use the left- and right-hand cord to tie one SK over all the cords. Make sure the left- and right-hand loops are of equal size. Tie an OHK on each cord, tightening the knot gently by pulling on each cord individually.

8 Thread on eight of the seed beads and tie OHKs on every cord about ³/₄ inch (1.9 cm) from the last OHK. Trim and attach an earring hook to the split ring. Repeat to make the other earring.

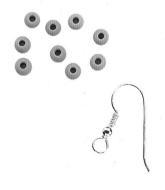

STONE DONUT EARRINGS
Small carnelian donuts display geometric knotting and a beaded tassel. Wirework forms a loop for attaching the earring hook.

INTERMEDIATE

WHAT YOU DO

1 Pin the first donut to your board. Double up three cords and LHK onto the donut. Beginning on the left side, use the right-hand cord as the filler cord and HCH over it with each cord in turn. Knot five rows, starting each time with the cord on the right side. Be sure to knot in the hanging filler cord from the previous row.

2 For the sixth row, begin with the filler cord from the right side and work toward the left. Repeat the same pattern from step 1 for five rows.

3 Beginning on the right side, repeat step 2. Then repeat step 1.

4 Bring all the cords together and tie two SKs with the left- and right-hand cords. Turn the earring over, and tie the two knotting cords you just used in an OHK up close to the SKs.

5 Thread on the seed beads and tie OHKs ½ inch (1.3 cm) from the knotting. Tie OHKs on the remaining cords.

6 Twist a small loop in the center of the wire. Curve one end through the donut and up, coiling the end. Coil the other end to hang in front. If the wire is too long, trim it slightly before coiling. Attach the earring hooks to the wire.

7 Repeat to make the other earring.

FINISHED LENGTH
2¾ inches (7 cm), not including hook

WHAT YOU NEED
12 natural linen cords, each 36 inches (91.4 cm) in length

2 1-inch (2.5 cm) carnelian stone donuts

14 carnelian seed beads, size 6

2 pieces of copper- or gold-colored wire, 3 inches (7.6 cm) in length

2 earring hooks

KNOTS USED
LHK—Lark's Head Knot (page 112)

HCH—Horizontal Clove Hitch (page 115)

SK—Square Knot (page 114)

OHK—Overhand Knot (page 113)

YELLOW EARRINGS WITH BEADED FRINGE
Make these rectangular earrings in different color combinations to match any outfit. There are three variations: without the fringe, with or without beads, and with a large flat bead attached by wire.

INTERMEDIATE

WHAT YOU DO

1 Draw a rectangle on the paper about the size you want your earring to be. My design measures ³/₄ x 1³/₄ inches (1.9 x 4.4 cm). Using five of the ten cords, find the center of one cord and tape it to the board, leaving a 2-inch (5.1 cm) space in the center. Find the center of each cord, double it up, and LHK it to the first cord. Pin each LHK to the board. Remove the tape and let the ends drop down.

2 With one cord of the embroidery floss, tape a 3-inch (7.6 cm) tail to the left side of the knotting. Using this cord, VCH each cord in turn, working from left to right. With the pin as a guide, reverse direction and VCH from right to left. Be sure to knot in the tail when you reach the left side. Continue knotting, adding new cords as needed or for color changes. Add a variety of beads as desired. Continue for 2¹/₂ inches (6.4 cm).

3 To finish off, tie a small OHK with some of the cords to hold the knotting in place. Tie an OHK on the two center cords ¹/₂ inch (1.3 cm) down from the knotting. Thread a seed bead on each of the other eight cords and tie an OHK under each bead. Trim.

4 Cut a piece of felt slightly smaller than the earring. Turn the earring over. Place a small hanger on the end of the earring with the loop extended and centered over the top edge. Spread a light amount of glue over the entire earring back. Put the felt on the earring and press down gently. Allow the earring to dry and then put on a hook.

VERSATILE BROOCH

INTERMEDIATE

You can turn this little brooch into a pendant just by stringing a cord of your choice through the opening in the aluminum tube. Use an "O" ring to keep the cords on, or glue a bead on the end.

WHAT YOU DO

1 Draw a 2 x 2-inch (5.1 x 5.1 cm) square on the paper on your board. Place "O" rings on the ends of the metal tube. Double one 18-inch green cord and LHK onto the tube. Pin each knot. Repeat with another 18-inch green cord and tie a SK with two filler cords. This will hold the cords tight. Repeat until you have seven SKs. Pin the tube and SKs to the board at the top of the square.

2 Tape a 3-inch (7.6 cm) "tail" from a medium green cord out to the left side. Use this cord as a knotting cord, tying VCHs over each cord from left to right. Turn the cord around the pin and knot from right to left for 21 knots. Place a seed bead on the next cord. Finish knotting the row. Remember to knot in any hanging cords as you come to them.

3 Take one of the turquoise cords and tie VCHs over the remaining cords to the left. Turn and knot from left to right. Tape the next six cords to the top of the board; these will hold the large oval bead.

4 Begin again on the left side with the first lavender cord, and be sure to tie in any hanging embroidery cords. VCH across to the space where the cords are lifted up. You will now be making VCHs in two separate areas to leave an empty space for the bead to hang. Turn the knotting board and tie three more VCHs.

5 Add in the chartreuse cord, knotting from right to left, turn and repeat from left to right, turn and tie six more VCHs. Add a seed bead on the next cord. Continue VCHs from right to left with an added turquoise cord. Turn and knot from left to right, then right to left, then turn and tie 14 more knots.

6 Pick up the lavender cord and tie two VCHs to the right, then turn and knot back to the left, and then to the right. On the left side, add another chartreuse cord. Knot VCHs from left to right, right to left, and left to right for seven knots. Take the lavender cord and VCH to the right, then turn and tie nine more VCHs to the left. Thread a seed bead on the next cord.

FINISHED LENGTH
$2^1/2$ x 3 inches (6.4 x 7.6 cm)

WHAT YOU NEED
2 rubber "O" rings to fit aluminum tubing

Aluminum tubing, 3 inches (7.6 cm) in diameter and $2^1/2$ inches (6.4 cm) in length

14 cords of green linen, each 18 inches (45.7 cm) in length

2 cords each of medium green, turquoise, lavender, and chartreuse cotton embroidery thread (cut more as needed), $1^1/2$ yards (1.4 m) in length

Approximately 30 seed beads in matching colors

5 cords of black cotton embroidery thread for accent, each 18 inches (45.7 cm) in length

Long oval bead, $1^1/4$ inches (3.2 cm) in diameter, for focal point

Pin back

KNOTS USED
SK—Square Knot (page 114)

LHK—Lark's Head Knot (page 112)

VCH—Vertical Clove Hitch (page 117)

HCH—Horizontal Clove Hitch (page 115)

OHK—Overhand Knot (page 113)

7 Start on the right again. VCH four knots from left to right with the turquoise cord. Thread a seed bead on two cords. Carry the turquoise cord down to the next row and VCH over three filler cords to the right.

8 Add a chartreuse cord on the right (add a new cord if necessary) and VCH from right to left and then back left to right. Knot four rows of VCHs. Add on a seed bead and finish the row with five more VCHs.

9 Take a lavender cord with a tail taped on the right. Knot VCHs from right to left. From left to right knot four VCHs, thread on a seed bead, and tie one more knot. Knot from right to left.

10 Pick up the chartreuse cord that was dropped in step 6, and pull the cord across the space left for the large oval bead. Continue knotting VCHs. Thread the large bead with the six cords taped up, pull down and VCH with chartreuse cord on the right side, then tie five knots from right to left. Pick up the turquoise cords and knot to the left side over all the cords. Turn the knotting board and knot once more from left to right across all cords.

11 Take the left-hand green filler cord, picking up any hanging embroidery cord ends, and HCH each filler cord over it in turn, working from left to right. Divide the hanging filler cords into groups of five, five, eight, five, and five cords. Tie an OHK with each group, including the turquoise embroidered cord in the last group. Trim that cord. Thread a seed bead onto each hanging cord, about ¾ inch (1.9 cm) down, securing the bead with an OHK. Trim.

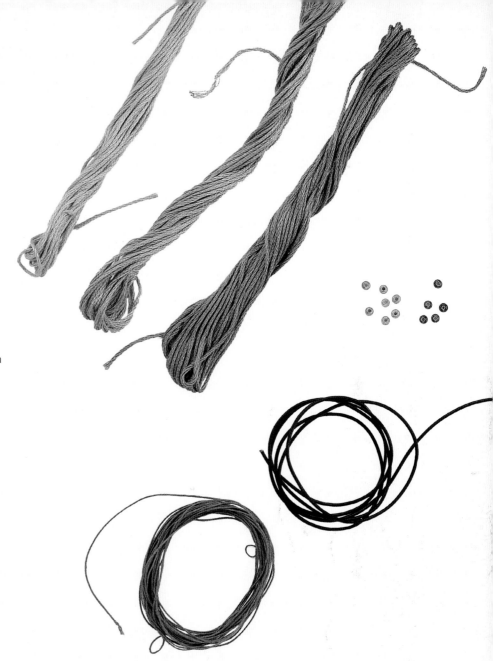

12 Tie an OHK with the five 18-inch (45.7 cm) pieces of the black cord. Trim the ends and pin it to the board. With the outside left- and right-hand cords, tie 4 inches (10.2 cm) of HKs. Pull the knotting through the space on the right at the top, leaving the knotted end in back. Weave the knotting in and out, over the middle of the tube and out and through the knotting. Tie an OHK on the end and leave about 1 inch (2.5 cm) of the ends free. Trim, letting the ends lie in front. Glue the pin back onto the back of the brooch.

DOUBLE DONUTS

H Here's a great way to use odd-sized donuts or rings: Double them up to make a fabulous pendant. Match them with some animal fetishes, Peruvian clay beads, glass arrowheads, or even your own clay fish toggle.

WHAT YOU DO

1 Find the center of six of the longer cords and tape them to your board. With the leftmost and rightmost cord, SK over the remaining four cords for about 1 inch (2.5 cm). Thread on one of the donuts (the smaller one if they are different sizes). Tie one tight SK over all ten cords with the top left- and right-hand cords. Set it aside.

2 Tape the other six long cords to the board. As above, SK for approximately 2 inches (5.1 cm) and thread on the other (larger, if applicable) donut at the opposite side of the other donut's knotting. With the left- and right-hand cord, SK over all ten cords in front of the knotting of the smaller donut. Continue SKs over all ten cords, holding the donut tightly, until you reach the end of the small donut's knotting. Pin the donuts and cords in place.

3 Thread all 24 cords through the large-holed ceramic bead. Divide the cords in half; then divide each half into three groups of four cords. Work on one side of the necklace at a time.

4 Using just the outside group of four cords, SK the left- and right-hand cords over the two filler cords for 2 inches (5.1 cm). Repeat SKs for 1¾ inches (4.4 cm) with the next group of four cords. Repeat SKs for 1½ inches (3.8 cm) with the inside group. This forms a slight curve in the necklace.

FINISHED LENGTH
22 inches (55.9 cm), not including pendant

WHAT YOU NEED
12 cords (of any fiber and color), each 10 feet (3 m) in length

8 cords (of the same material), each 1½ yards (1.4 m) in length

Ceramic bead with large hole

2 round ceramic beads, each ½ inch (1.3 cm) in diameter

2 stone donuts or rings

2 carved animal fetishes

2 arrowhead beads (or any dangle beads)

2 disk beads

30 seed beads, size 6

2 pony beads

2 head pins

Toggle

Needle or wire

KNOTS USED
HK—Half Knot (page 113)

SK—Square Knot (page 114)

HCH—Horizontal Clove Hitch (page 115)

SKP—Square Knot Picot (page 39)

OHK—Overhand Knot (page 113)

ASK—Alternating Square Knot (see step 3, page 43)

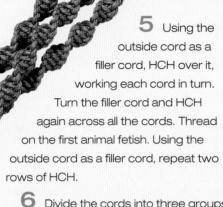

5 Using the outside cord as a filler cord, HCH over it, working each cord in turn. Turn the filler cord and HCH again across all the cords. Thread on the first animal fetish. Using the outside cord as a filler cord, repeat two rows of HCH.

6 Divide the cords into three groups of four. With one group, tie four SKs with the left- and right-hand cords over the two remaining filler cords. Repeat with the other two groups. Leaving two cords out on each side, tie four ASKs with the remaining two groups. Before beginning the third row of ASKs, thread on the first arrowhead or dangle bead. Continue with one more row of ASKs for each of the three groups of four. (You will put on the overlay knotting later.)

7 Pin down the knotting. Knot two rows of HCH as you did in step 5, using one outside cord as a filler cord. Thread one of the two ceramic beads onto the middle cord. Continue with one row of HCH across all the cords. Continue HCHs back and forth for 15 more rows.

8 Thread on the first small seed bead on top of the disk bead with a head pin. Push the head pin through the HCH rows at the desired place, clip it, and coil.

TIP
Build this necklace from the front to the back.

9 Divide the cords into two groups. Thread one of the 1½-yard (1.4 m) cords on the needle or wire and pull it through the knotting on the last row of HCH, just above the animal bead on the right-hand side, about ⅛ inch (3 mm) from the edge. Thread another 1½-yard (1.4 m) cord about the same distance from the first cord. Repeat on the other side. You should now have four cords hanging on each side on top of the ASKs. With the left- and right-hand cords, tie one SK over the two filler cords.

10 Tie a SKP, adding one seed bead on the outside cord of the SK, leaving a loop on the other side. Make seven of these knots. Repeat with the other four cords.

11 Use the needle to pull each of these cords between the next two rows of HCHs. Turn over the necklace and, using these same two groups of four cords, tie two rows of four SKs.

12 Using the needle again, pull the cords up through the right side of the necklace between the next two rows of HCHs. Tie an OHK with the first two cords, leaving out a left- and right-hand cord, and repeat with the other two sets of two cords, about ¼ inch (6 mm) down. Bring the outer cords down and tie OHKs in four groups of two cords. Repeat for the first and second rows.

13 Divide the top and bottom cords into two groups of eight cords. With the left- and right-hand cords from one group, HK over the six filler cords. Continue for 1½ inches (3.8 cm), gradually cutting out four of the filler cords. Repeat with the other group. Thread on the first pony bead. Finish with a loop or toggle bead.

14 Repeat steps 4 to 13 to form the other side of the necklace.

OCEAN WAVE
Necklace

INTERMEDIATE

T he blue-green water and white frothy waves on these heart-shaped glass beads by Mary Jarvis call for multicolored strands of cords and wavy lines. The shiny 2-mm cord and coordinating ribbon yarn enhances the ocean feeling.

WHAT YOU DO

1 Thread one 3-yard (2.7 m) cord through the bead to the center. Thread another 3-yard (2.7 m) cord through the loop, center it, and double it. You now have three cords to knot with. Keeping one cord as a filler cord, AHH around the filler cord with the left-hand cord. Repeat with the right-hand cord. Continue alternating these knots for 2½ inches (6.4 cm).

2 Thread on one of the pony beads. Keeping one cord as a filler cord, SK with the left- and right-hand cords for 2½ inches (6.4 cm). Thread on the first medium-sized bead.

3 Continue AHHs as in step 1 for 3½ inches (8.9 cm). Tie one SK.

4 Start again on the other side of the focal bead. Repeating step 2, SK for 2½ inches (6.4 cm). Thread on the second medium-sized bead.

5 Using one cord as a filler cord, SK with the left- and right-hand cords for 2½ inches (6.4 cm). Thread on another pony bead.

6 Repeat step 3. Both sides should now be the same length. If not, add a knot or two to even them up.

7 Pin the ends of the necklace securely to your board. Take the longest cord from one end of the necklace. This will form another necklace strand (and will end up tied in an OHK on the other side of the necklace). Thread on the assorted colors of beads, one every 2 to 3 inches (5.1 to 7.6 cm), and secure them in place with an OHK underneath. Position the strand slightly overlapping the focal bead.

TIP
The author made a matching fish toggle to go with the theme of the necklace. If you'd like to do the same, use clay or polymer clay.

FINISHED LENGTH
28 inches (71.7 cm)

WHAT YOU NEED
3 multi-colored cords (2 mm in diameter), each 3 yards (2.7 m) in length

2 pieces of matching multi-colored ribbon yarn, each 2 yards (1.8 m) in length

Large focal bead with horizontal hole

26 pony beads (or other same-size beads with large holes)

2 medium-sized, matching beads

Toggle

4-inch (10.2 cm) piece of 18- or 20-gauge wire

KNOTS USED
SK—Square Knot (page 114)

HK—Half Knot (page 113)

OHK—Overhand Knot (page 113)

AHH—Alternating Half Hitch (page 114)

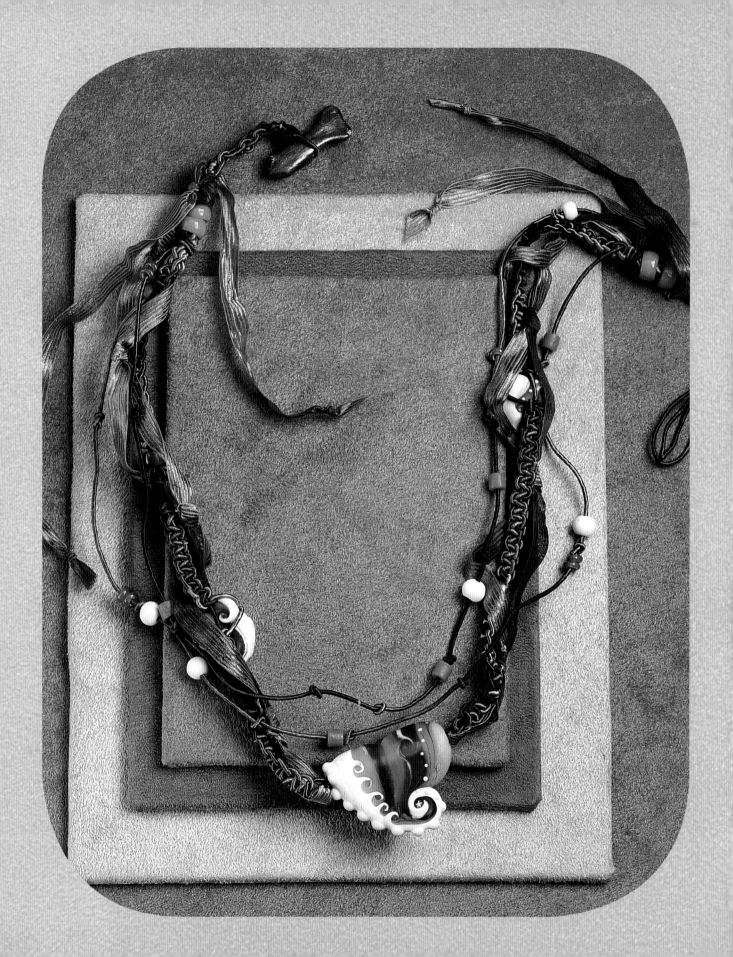

8 On the opposite side, hold out one long cord. Tie an OHK with the two remaining cords. Pull the knot tightly, clip off the shortest cord, and place a dab of glue on the knot. Allow the glue to dry. Take the remaining cord and repeat, adding on more beads. Try to not place the beads in the same place as a bead from the first strand.

9 On the toggle side, thread on two pony beads, run cords through the toggle, and finish as usual. For the "loop" side, make a loop with the two cords, tie an OHK, and finish off with SKs.

10 Thread one length of ribbon yarn through the wire loop on one side of the focal bead, using a wire needle to pull the yarn through the loop. Center the yarn and double it up. Keeping the yarn slightly twisted and loose, tie an OHK about 2 inches (5.1 cm) from the focal bead. Continue tying knots behind and in front of the main knotted cord, ending just above the last pony beads. Wrap the yarn around the necklace for two turns and tie a SK without fillers. Cut off the ends of the yarn at about 6 inches (15.2 cm), tying an OHK on the ends. Tuck the ends in between the other cords and allow them to hang loose. Repeat on the other side.

CARVED STONE PENDANT

INTERMEDIATE

This monochromatic, multi-strand necklace contains a variety of ethnic beads. The pendant is quite heavy, but stringing beading wire in the black section of the necklace helps carry the weight.

BLACK STRAND
You make this necklace in three separate strands: this Black Strand, and the Gray Strand and Gray Tape Yarn Strand that follow.

WHAT YOU DO

1 Thread the beading wire through the loop of the toggle. Crimp and trim it. Thread the four black cords through the toggle to the center and double them up around the wire. You will enclose the wire in the knotting. Tie 2½ inches (6.4 cm) of SKs over all the cords, using the outside left- and right-hand cords.

2 Thread the first black bead onto the end of the knotting. Tie AHHs for 2½ inches (6.4 cm) with the outside cords. Tie one SK.

3 Thread the first agate bead onto the two center cords and wire. If the two cords won't fit through the bead, just use the wire. Using the three cords on the left side, HK with the outer left- and outer right-hand cords over the one filler cord for 1 inch (2.5 cm). (This must be enough knotting to go around one side of the agate bead.) Repeat with the three cords on the right side. Tie one SK with the two outside cords over all the filler cords.

4 Divide the cords into two groups of four, including the wire in one group. Tie 2 inches (5.1 cm) of HKs using the outside cords from the left-hand group as knotting cords. Repeat on the right side. Bring all the cords together and, with a left- and right-hand cord, tie one SK over all the filler cords.

TIP
To prepare the pendant, fold the silver wire in half. Thread the center end through the pendant's hole and up over the top. Pull the wires through the loop and curl the ends into small coils. Clip off any excess wire before coiling.

FINISHED LENGTH
24 inches (61 cm)

WHAT YOU NEED
#49 beading wire, 28 inches (71.1 cm) in length

Button for toggle

2 crimps

4 cords of 5-ply black linen, each 3 yards (2.7 m) in length

2 round black wood beads with large holes, ½ inch (1.3 cm) in diameter

2 agate beads, ¾ inch (1.9 cm) in diameter

#18 silver wire, 4 inches (10.2 cm) in length

1 large pendant

4 horn beads, 1 inch (2.5 cm) in diameter

2 Krobo or other glass beads, ¾ inch (1.9 cm) in diameter

KNOTS USED
SK—Square Knot (page 114)

HK—Half Knot (page 113)

AHH—Alternating Half Hitch (page 114)

OHK—Overhand Knot (page 113)

5 Divide the cords into two groups again and thread a horn bead on each. Bringing all the cords together, tie AHHs for 1 1/2 inches (3.8 cm) using the outside left- and right-hand cords.

6 Thread on the first Krobo glass bead. Tie HKs over all the cords for 1 inch (2.5 cm). Thread the cords through the pendant loops and repeat HKs for 1 inch (2.5 cm). Thread on the second Krobo glass bead. Reverse the board and knot the other side.

7 Repeat step 5, tying AHHs and threading on the horn beads. Repeat the rest of the directions and thread on the other black bead. Make a small loop on the end of the beading wire, 2 inches (5.1 cm) from the bead. Crimp, and you're done working on this section of the necklace.

GRAY STRAND

WHAT YOU DO

1 Lay the beads out on your paper with your necklace. Position them in between the areas in the black knotting with no beads. On the toggle side of the necklace, push up one of the black, large-holed beads. Using a wire needle, pull the three cords through the knotting, under where the black bead will lie. Pull down the black bead and double up the cords. Using a left- and right-hand cord as knotting cords, knot to center using groups of HKs and SKs. The cylinder bead in the center should lie just above the pendant wire. As you work, pull the gray knotting in between the section of black knotting where there are two separate cords.

2 When your knotting reaches the end of the black section, trim two cords from the center of the knotting. Trim four cords from the filler cords of the black section. Put a light dab of glue on the trimmed ends. Thread all the cords through the large black bead. Thread three black cord ends through the loop in the beading wire to hold it firmly in place. Using two black cords over the remaining cord, make a toggle loop as usual, knotting over the wire.

WHAT YOU NEED

3 cords of 3-ply gray linen, each 3 1/3 yards (3 m) in length

2 black clay bird beads, 1/2 to 3/4 inch (1.3 to 1.9 cm)

Carved bone bead

2 small agate beads

White ceramic bead

Black cylinder bead, 1 inch (2.5 cm) in diameter

2 small black disks

Wire needle

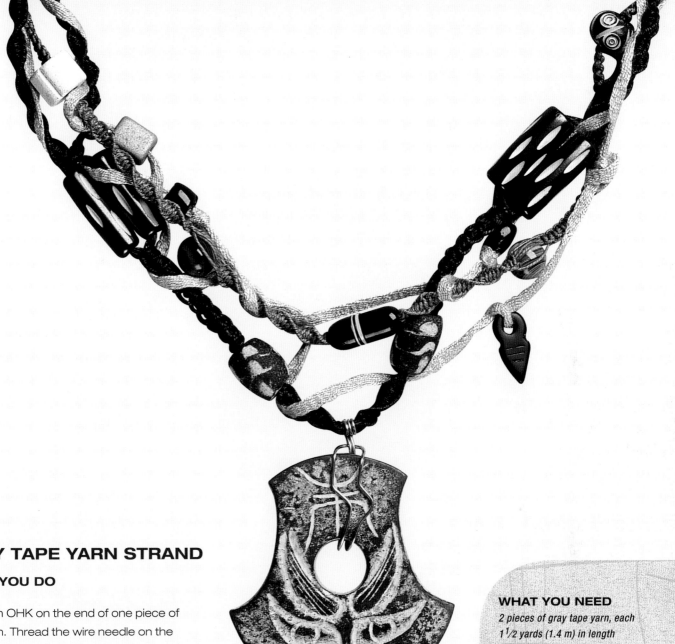

GRAY TAPE YARN STRAND

WHAT YOU DO

1 Tie an OHK on the end of one piece of tape yarn. Thread the wire needle on the other end and pull the yarn through the large-holed black bead on the toggle end of the necklace. Before pulling the knot inside the bead, put a dab of glue on it. Loosely loop the yarn through the necklace, adding the beads and small OHKs as needed. When you reach the black bead on the other end of the necklace, put some glue on the part of the yarn that will go inside the bead. Pull it through and trim.

2 Repeat with the second piece of tape yarn, starting at the loop end of the necklace.

WHAT YOU NEED

2 pieces of gray tape yarn, each 1 1/2 yards (1.4 m) in length

6 small-to-medium gray and black beads

Wire needle

TIP

You will loosely weave these two pieces of yarn in and out of the sections of the necklace, placing the six beads where needed to fill gaps, and tying decorative knots to fill up any leftover spaces.

SHOWCASE PENDANT

ADVANCED

This colorful glass bead and the multicolored tape yarn look like they were made for each other. Vertical Clove Hitches provide a soft textured background that sets off the focal bead worn as a pendant.

WHAT YOU DO

1 Pin the neckwire to the board. Double the first brown 22-inch (55.9 cm) cord and LHK it onto the wire. Repeat with the remainder of the 22-inch (55.9 cm) cords, and pin the knots to the board. Leave a small space between each knot. (If needed, tie SKs with each set of the four cords to hold them in place.)

2 Tape a 3-inch (7.6 cm) tail out of the first 1½-yard (1.4 m) yarn pieces to the left-hand side and VCH over each cord in turn from left to right. Turn and VCH back from right to left. Continue this knotting, adding on new cords as needed, until you have knotted 2 inches (5.1 cm).

3 Begin decreasing knotting and leave a cord out on each side. Start with the second cord from the left, and leave out the last cord on the right. Continue this pattern, leaving out a cord on each side for five rows. Use the first cord you left out as a filler cord, and HCH each left-out cord over it in turn, following the slant of the knotting. After each cord is knotted, include it as a filler cord. Repeat on the other side.

4 Turn the necklace over. Wrap the 12-inch (30.5 cm) piece of yarn around the cords, tying a Binding Knot. Pull each cord gently to straighten the knot. Thread a seed bead on each cord 1½ inches (3.8 cm) from the Binding Knot. Tie an OHK to hold the bead in place and trim.

5 LHK the 30-inch (76.2 cm) piece of yarn over the center LHK. Tie an OHK and thread the cords through the flat focal bead. Tie another OHK to hold the bead in place. Tie OHKs in each cord and trim at the level of the tassel cords.

FINISHED LENGTH

5 inches (12.7 cm) to the end of the tassel

WHAT YOU NEED

Silver neckwire, 16- or 20-gauge

9 cords of dark brown cotton, each 22 inches (55.9 cm) in length

Multicolored tape yarn:
   5 pieces each 1½ yards (1.4 m) long
   1 piece, 12 inches (30.5 cm) long
   1 piece, 30 inches (76.2 cm) long

16 bronze seed beads, size 6

Large flat focal bead, 1¾ inches (4.4 cm) in diameter

KNOTS USED

LHK—Lark's Head Knot (page 112)

SK—Square Knot (page 114)

VCH—Vertical Clove Hitch (page 117)

HCH—Horizontal Clove Hitch (page 115)

BK—Binding Knot (page 118)

OHK—Overhand Knot (page 113)

CAVANDOLI PENDANT

ADVANCED

SILVER CHARMS BY LOIS VENARCHICK

Cavandoli knotting—created in Turin, Italy, by a school principal—produces a geometric pattern using two colors of strong, smooth cord like linen or cotton. This technique even produces an attractive pattern underneath as well.

WHAT YOU DO

1 Draw a 2 x 2¼-inch (5.1 x 5.7 cm) rectangle on paper on your board. Tape all the 2-yard (1.8 m) Color A cords to the board at the top of the rectangle. Beginning on the left side, HK with the left- and right-hand cords over the four other (filler) cords, from the edge of the rectangle to the end of the cords—16 inches (40.6 cm) of knotting in all. Tie an OHK. Using each cord in turn, thread on a seed bead and tie an OHK under each bead, leaving a space of 2 inches (5.1 cm) from the end of the knotting to the seed bead. Trim the cords. Repeat on the right side. Be sure to switch knotting cords as needed.

2 Double up the 11 cords of Color B in turn. LHK each to the center section of the cords on your board. Pin each LHK to the board.

3 Tape a tail of one of the 1½-yard (1.4 m) Color A cords to the left side of your board. Tie VCHs across. Pin down the knotting as needed, following the rectangle guidelines.

4 Turn the cord and, using the same cord as a filler cord, HCH each hanging cord over the filler cord from right to left.

5 Take the color A knotting cord, use it as a filler cord, and knot each hanging cord over it in turn.

6 Tie four VCHs with the same cord (cord A) from right to left (R>L). Knot two HCHs with the hanging cords. Then tie 16 VCHs with cord A.

TIP
This type of knotting works well with a graph pattern where each square equals one knot. Follow the colors of the pattern with your knotting!

FINISHED LENGTH
34 inches (86.4 cm)

WHAT YOU NEED
Cords of cotton, as follows:
6 cords in Color A (maroon),
each 2 yards (1.8 m) in length
11 cords in Color B (lavender),
each 24 inches (61 cm) in length
3 cords in Color A (maroon), each
1½ yards (1.4 m) in length

Approximately 80 gray and maroon seed beads, size 6

2 silver charms

Tiny silver bead

2 head pins

Thread in matching color

KNOTS USED
LHK—Lark's Head Knot (page 112)

HK—Half Knot (page 113)

OHK—Overhand Knot (page 113)

HCH—Horizontal Clove Hitch (page 115)

VCH—Vertical Clove Hitch (page 117)

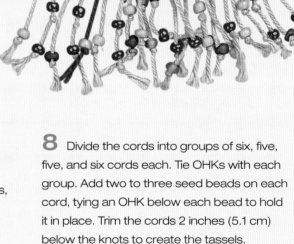

7 In the following directions, knot the VCHs with the maroon cord A and the HCHs with the lavender cord B. Add on a new 1½-yard (1.4 m) cord as needed. Practicing this will enable you to follow a graph.

L>R: 3 VCHs, 2 HCHs, and 4 VCHs

R>L: 4 VCHs, add 1 bead, skip that cord, 2 HCHs, 9 VCHs, add 1 bead, skip that cord, and 3 VCHs

L>R: 3 VCHs, 2 HCHs, 9 VCHs, and 2 VCHs

R>L: 4 VCHs, 2 HCHs, 16 VCHs

L>R: 11 VCHs, add 1 bead, 4 VCHs, 2 HCHs, and 4 VCHs

R>L: 10 VCHs, add 1 bead, and 11 VCHs

L>R: VCH across

R>L: 2 VCHs, 2 HCHs, and 18 VCHs

L>R: 17 VCHs, 3 HCHs, and 2 VCHs

R>L: 2 VCHs, 4 HCHs, and 16 VCHs

L>R: 15 VCHs, 5 HCHs, and 2 HCHs

R>L: 2 VCHs, 6 HCHs, and 14 VCHs

L>R: 1 VCH, add 1 bead, 13 VCHs, 5 HCHs, and 2 VCHs

R>L: 2 VCHs, 4 HCHs, and 16 VCHs

L>R: 17 VCHs, 3 HCHs, and 2 VCHs

R>L: 2 VCHs, 2 HCHs, and 18 VCHs

L>R: 22 VCHs

R>L: 22 HCHs

8 Divide the cords into groups of six, five, five, and six cords each. Tie OHKs with each group. Add two to three seed beads on each cord, tying an OHK below each bead to hold it in place. Trim the cords 2 inches (5.1 cm) below the knots to create the tassels.

9 Secure the two charms in place by threading a head pin through the charms' holes and through the knotting. Finish off the head pin in the back with a wire coil. Tie in the single silver bead with a thread.

STRANDS OF PLUM

ADVANCED

DICHROIC BEADS BY PAULA RADKE

Silver cones hide the cord ends in this multi-strand necklace, and the chain contributes to the look. I used antique, vintage, and Bali silver beads, but you can create your own combination. The dichroic beads add sparkle to the raspberry color of the cords.

WHAT YOU DO

1 At the end of a piece of the wire, make a 4-mm loop. Thread the five cords through the loop to the center and double them up. Pull the wire through one of the cones, making sure all the cords fit, and form a loop at the narrow end of the cone. Pin the loop to your board.

2 Pick up three cords and tape the others out of the way. Using the outermost left- and right-hand cord, tie HKs for 3 inches (7.6 cm) over one filler cord, beginning inside the cone. Thread on a silver bead, knot 2 inches (5.1 cm), and thread on another silver bead. Knot 2 more inches (5.1 cm) and thread on a dichroic bead. Knot for 1½ inches (3.8 cm) and thread on one of the larger silver beads. Knot 2 more inches (5.1 cm) and then thread on a large cylinder bead.

3 Turn the board and knot 2 inches (5.1 cm). Thread on the other larger silver bead. Knot 1½ inches (3.8 cm) and thread on a silver bead. Knot 2 inches (5.1 cm) and thread on a dichroic bead. Knot 2½ inches and thread on a silver bead. Knot 3 inches (7.6 cm) or until the knotting is even with where you began knotting. Tape down the end.

TIP

After you finish knotting the first group of cords, tape the end of the knotting to the top of your board, even with where you began knotting. This will serve as a guideline for the rest of the cords. Save the two shorter cords until the end.

FINISHED LENGTH

30 inches (76.2 cm), 5 inches (12.7 cm) from cone to toggle

WHAT YOU NEED

2 lengths of 20-gauge sterling silver wire, each 3 inches (7.6 cm) in length

5 cords of cotton/rayon in raspberry, each 4 yards (3.7 m) in length

1 cord of cotton/rayon in raspberry, 2½ yards (2.3 m) in length

2 large silver cones with an opening of at least ¼ inch (6 mm)

10 assorted small silver beads

9 disk-shaped dichroic beads

2 silver beads, about ½ inch (1.3 cm) in length

2 long silver beads, 1 inch (2.5 cm) in length

3 silver Bali beads

4 6-mm jump rings

Silver toggle

Silver chain, 6 inches (15.2 cm) in length

KNOTS USED

HK—Half Knot (page 113)

AHH—Alternating Half Hitch (page 114)

OHK—Overhand Knot (page 113)

4 HK the next three cords, using the knotting you did in steps 2 and 3 as a guide. Knot this group over the first group, placing the central cylinder bead just above the center bead in the first group. Follow these knotting instructions: Knot 3½ inches (8.9 cm) and thread on a dichroic bead. Knot 1½ inches (3.8 cm) and thread on a silver bead. Knot 2 inches (5.1 cm) and add on another silver bead. Knot 2½ inches and add on the center bead.

> **TIP**
>
> You should consider the lengths specified in step 4 as just guidelines. Adjust to the length of your actual work.

5 Turn your work and knot 2½ inches (6.4 cm). Thread on a dichroic bead. Knot 1½ inches more, and then thread on a silver Bali bead. Knot 2½ inches. Thread on a Bali silver bead. Then continue to knot until you reach the ends of the knotting you did in step 3.

6 With two cords, tie AHHs for 5 inches (12.7 cm). Thread on a silver bead, knot for 3 inches (7.6 cm), thread on a dichroic bead, and knot 3 more inches (7.6 cm). Thread on another dichroic bead—these beads should lie on either side of the central beads. Knot 4½ inches (11.4 cm) and thread on another silver Bali bead. Again, continue knotting until you reach the end.

7 With two more of the longer cords, tie AHHs, adding in three dichroic and three silver beads in places where needed.

8 Using a short strand, tie OHKs at intervals of 2 to 3 inches (5.1 to 7.6 cm). Repeat with the last strand.

9 Cut out the middle cord and apply glue to the two groups of three knotted cords. Let them dry. Tie an OHK with the four ends left. Tie an OHK with the two groups of two cords. Tie an OHK in the two single cords. Make a curve in the end of the last strand of wire. Thread it through the cords and make the loop tight to hold. Trim the ends of the cords to about ¼ inch. Pull the wire through the cone and make a loop on the other end.

10 Using the jump rings, attach the chain to the cone ends and the other end to the toggles.

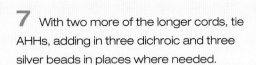

CHUNKY GOLD NET
Necklace

ADVANCED

I designed this necklace especially for tape yarns. It is very full, but lightweight, and it features gold upon gold upon gold. I even made my own polymer clay cones and a bead to match. An old button serves as the toggle.

WHAT YOU DO

1 Thread four cords of the tape yarn through the button loop and double them up. With an outside left- and right-hand cord, SK over all the cords for 4 inches (10.2 cm). Thread the cords through the first cone. Push the cone temporarily back onto the knotting.

2 With the remaining four cords of the tape yarn, find the center and lay them directly over the area where the cone will lie. Lay the four silk cords on top. Pull two cords from the first group around all the cords and tie a SK on top with no fillers. Drop down all the cords and pull the cone over the knot.

3 Combine one silk cord with every other cord, tying an OHK with every two cords (including the silk cord) across. Tie the knots 1¼ inch (3.2 cm) down from the cone.

4 Leave a cord out on each side (alternating the rows of knots). Thread a pony bead on the next two cords and tie an OHK 1 inch (2.5 cm) down from the row above. Repeat for two more rows.

5 Gather all the cords together 1 inch (2.5 cm) down and then thread them through the large-holed bead. If the hole is large enough, tie an OHK and tighten by pulling gently on each cord in turn. Push the knot inside the bead.

6 Repeat steps 4 and 5, knotting four rows and threading on beads. Cut off the silk cord above the last knots. Leave out one cord and then tie an OHK with all the other cords where you will place the cone. Pin the necklace on your board, making sure that the sides match up.

7 Finish off the cords by making a loop for the button as usual. Take the remaining cord and weave it through the open sides of the knotting to hold it together. Use a needle for this, threading the cord through the center bead. Continue weaving in and out on the other side. End by tying it onto a cord just before the first cone.

FINISHED LENGTH
22 inches (55.9 cm)

WHAT YOU NEED
8 cords of gold tape yarn, each 3 yards (2.7 m) in length

4 cords of gold silk yarn, each 1½ yards (1.4 m) in length

Button for toggle

2 large cone beads, 1 inch (2.5 cm) in length

44 gold-colored pony beads

Large-holed bead, 1¼ inch (3.2 cm) in length

Needle

KNOTS USED
SK—Square Knot (page 114)

OHK—Overhand Knot (page 113)

TIP
If the knot is too large for the cone, pull half the cords through the cone and tie a knot in the rest that you can then push into the cone.

STONES, BONES & FOSSILS

ADVANCED

This necklace lets you show off some items you can't string on a cord. They don't have to be the same ones I used—just try to find similar shapes and sizes. The pendant's large hole provides an easy way to begin knotting, but you can also use a wire loop.

WHAT YOU DO

1 Thread three pieces of the 3½-yard (3.2 m) cord through the hole in the pendant. Double up the cords and tie an OHK with all the cords. Pin the pendant to the top of your board. Divide the cords into two even groups. In the left group, use a left-hand cord and a right-hand cord to tie two SKs over the center filler cord. Repeat in the group on the right. Leaving out a left- and right-hand cord, tie a SK with the four center cords, adding in two more 3½-yard (3.2 m) cords.

> ### TIP
> Making a longer necklace like this one enables you to easily slip it over your head.

2 Divide the cords into two groups of three and one group of four, with the group of four in the middle. In each group, use a left- and right-hand cord to tie two SKs. The two groups of three will have one filler cord, while the other group will have two. Tie seven rows of two ASKs each. When you reach the seventh row, thread one cord through the hole in the fish pendant, and then finish knotting. If you need another cord to hold the fish in place, use a scrap of cord and tie the fish to the knotting, ending with an OHK in back. Clip and pull the ends out of sight. Then trim the knots.

3 Pin down the knotting. HCH each cord over the right-hand cord as a filler cord, working from right to left. Knot two more rows of HCHs. Thread the two outside cords through the cylinder bead from opposite sides. If the cords will not fit, insert a headpin, making a loop for the cord on either end. Run other cords underneath and repeat the three rows of HCHs.

FINISHED LENGTH
28 inches (71.1 cm)

WHAT YOU NEED
Cords of natural linen (or hemp), as follows:

> 5 cords, each 3½ yards (3.2 m) in length
> 8 cords, each 1½ yards (1.4 m) in length

Stone (jasper) pendant, 1½ x 3 inches (3.8 x 7.6 cm)

Fish pendant (jasper or bone), 2 inches (5.1 cm) in length

Cylinder "bamboo" bead (serpentine), 1½ inch (3.2 cm) in length

Rectangular stone (jasper) donut, 1¼ x 2 inches (3.2 x 5.1 cm)

2 pieces of fossilized sea urchin, ¾ inch (1.9 cm) in length

2 pieces of fossilized sea urchin, 1 inch (2.5 cm) in length

4 pony beads, of a matching color

Stone donut landscape (jasper), 1¼ inch (3.2 cm) in length

Large stone (onyx) bead, ¾ inch (1.9 cm) in length

Squared stone (jasper), 1 inch (2.5 cm) in length

Petrified palm wood disk, 1 inch (2.5 cm) in diameter

4 Divide the cords into two groups of three and one group of four, with the group of four in the middle. Using the outermost left and right cords of the first group of three (on the left), tie six HKs with one filler cord. Repeat with the group of four, using two filler cords. Finish with the last group, again using only one filler cord. Leaving a cord out on each side, tie two sets of AHKs with two filler cords each. Leave out one middle cord and thread on the rectangular stone, adding a cord back into the knotting. Complete five rows of AHKs.

5 Pin down your knotting. HCH each cord over the left cord as a filler cord. Turn the knotting and tie one more row. Thread the two small pieces of sea urchin spine onto a center cord, bring all the cords down, and repeat two rows of HCHs. Divide the cords into two groups of five cords, threading the two center cords through the large sea urchin bead.

6 Take the outer cords of the left group and tie HKs for 1 inch (2.5 cm). Repeat on the other side. Add in the two center cords and HK for ³/₄ inch (1.9 cm). Thread on the first pony bead and HK for 1 more inch (2.5 cm). Cut out all but four of the cords. Put a dab of glue on the cut ends and let them dry. Thread on the second pony bead. Thread the cords through the donut and knot back 1¼ inches (3.2 cm) to the pony bead. End as usual.

7 Begin working on the opposite side of the necklace. Thread the four 1½-yard (1.4 m) cords through the pendant to the center. Double up the cords and tie an OHK tight up against the pendant. Divide the cords into two groups of four cords. Tie ³/₄ inch (1.9 cm) of HKs with the outside cords of the left-hand group. Thread on the onyx bead with the large hole. With four cords, knot SKs for 2½ inches (6.4 cm) over the two outer cords as knotting cords. Thread the knotting through the lower end of the rectangular stone donut and knot over the first knotting, back to the onyx bead. Cut out the two filler cords. Tie a SK without fillers and pull the end through the bead as usual.

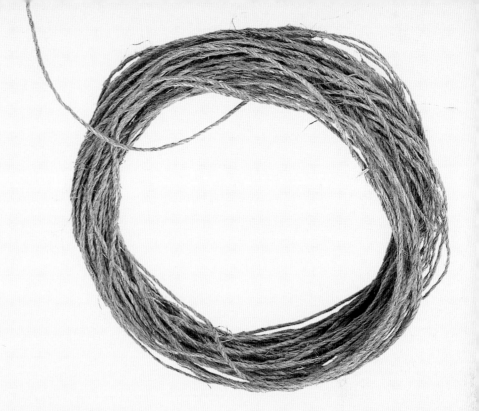

8 With the other four cords—knotting with the two outer cords and using the two inner cords as filler cords—HK for 4 inches (10.2 cm). Twist this cord around the SK knotting and end by cutting out the filler cords and using the wire needle to pull the ends through the knotting by the stone, and tying an OHK. Tuck the ends inside and trim.

9 Begin again on the other side of the rectangle. LHK the four 1½-yard-long (1.4 m) cords together on the rectangular stone donut. Repeat with the four remaining cords. HCH each cord in turn over a right-hand cord as a filler cord. Turn and knot one more row. Using two middle cords, thread through the palm wood disk. Repeat for two rows of HCHs.

10 Divide the cords into two groups of seven and one group of two, with the group of two in the middle. With a left- and right-hand cord in the left-most group of seven, tie 1¾ inches (4.4 cm) of SKs. Repeat on the right side (the other group of seven). Tie AHHs with the cords in the center group for 1¾ inches (4.4 cm). Pin it all down.

11 Using the left-hand cord as a filler cord, HCH across and back. Divide the cords into two groups of seven and one group of two, with the group of two in the middle. In the first group of seven (on the left), tie HKs for 1¼ inches (3.2 cm). Repeat with the other group of seven (on the right). Thread the center cords through the sea urchin spine bead. Bring all the cords together. Using left- and right-hand cords, tie HKs for ¾ inch (1.9 cm) and thread on the first pony bead. HK for 1 inch (2.5 cm). Cut out all but four of the cords. Put a dab of glue on the cord ends and let them dry. Thread the cords through the donut and SK for 1¼ inches (3.2 cm) to the pony bead. End as usual.

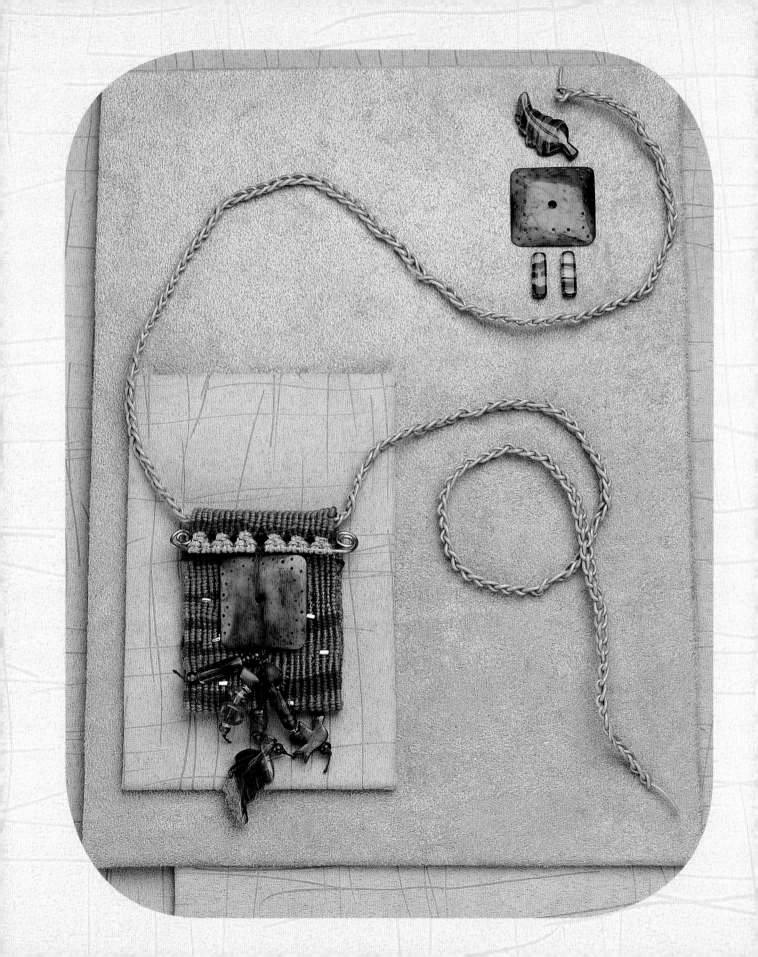

AUTUMN GOLD
Purse
ADVANCED

Y You make this little purse, which you can also wear as a necklace, by knotting leather on a wire, folding it over, and sewing up the sides. You can easily change the purse's size to fit your needs.

WHAT YOU DO

1 Draw a rectangle on your paper measuring 2¼ x 6 inches (5.7 x 15.2 cm). This is the area that you will clove hitch. The first ¾ inch (1.9 cm) will become the flap. Divide the rest of the rectangle into two sections: the back of the purse and the front.

2 Measure 2¼ inches (5.7 cm) of wire in the center. Coil up the ends to that point. LHK one of the 24-inch (61 cm) cords onto the wire on the left. Repeat with another 24-inch (61 cm) cord. With the outside left and outside right cords, tie a SK. Repeat with the rest of the cords. Pin it just above the rectangle.

3 Tape a tail from one of the cotton embroidery cords out to the left and VCH across to the right side. Now decide how you want the colors to look. You can vary the colors or add in different amounts. You can end a color in the middle or off to one side. It's up to you.

4 Continue knotting, keeping within the lines of the diagram, until you have completed 6 inches (15.2 cm). Remember to include all the hanging ends in the knotting as you go.

5 Trim the edges of the filler cords and knotting cords to ½ inch (1.3 cm). Fold the ends over and place some glue underneath. When it's dry, place a small amount of glue on the felt and place it over the ends. Let it dry.

Special Knot: CK—Chain Knot
This knot is formed with one cord. Tie a small loop on the end of a cord. Pull a small loop through this loop. Continue pulling small loops through the previous loop, tightening as needed. To end, pull the cord entirely through the previous loop and tighten.

FINISHED LENGTH
2¼ x 3 inches (5.7 x 7.6 cm)

WHAT YOU NEED
18-gauge brass wire, 5 inches (12.7 cm) in length

12 natural linen cords, each 24 inches (61 cm) in length

6 cords each of four colors (24 cords total) embroidery cotton, each 1½ yards (1.4 m) in length (I used gold, tan, brown, and green.)

Piece of felt or leather, ½ x 2 inches (1.3 x 5.1 cm)

Strong thread of a matching color

Gold leather cord, 3 yards (2.7 m) in length

Bone, 1 x 1¼ inches (2.5 x 3.2 cm)

20 square gold seed beads, size 6

3 amber nuggets

Agate leaf

2 cylindrical, striped gold CZ glass beads, ¾ inch (1.9 cm) in length

Green jasper bird

8 assorted glass beads

KNOTS USED
LHK—Lark's Head Knot (page 112)

SK—Square Knot (page 114)

VCH—Vertical Clove Hitch (page 117)

OHK—Overhand Knot (page 113)

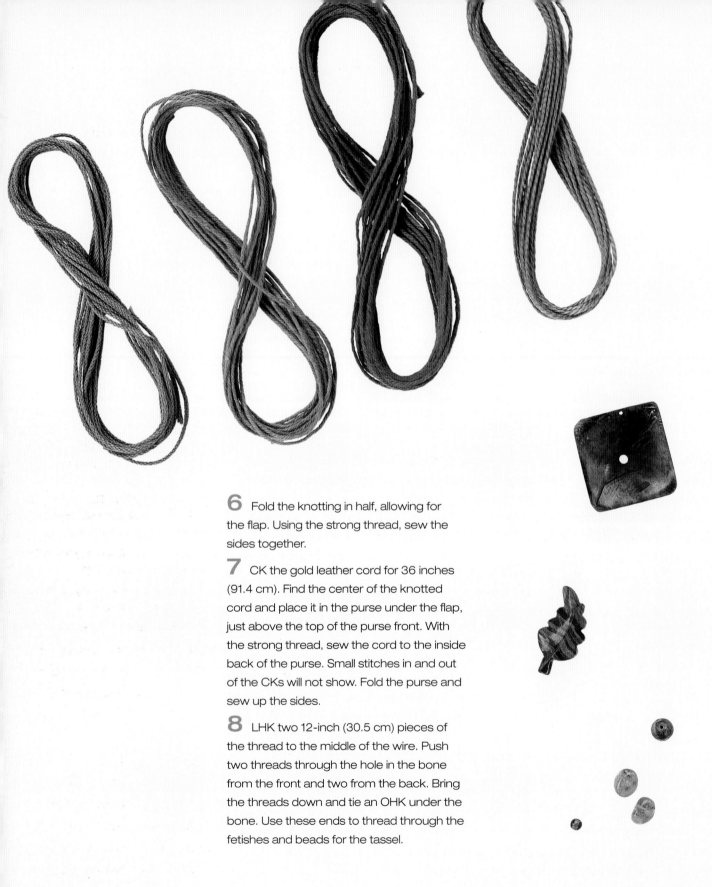

6 Fold the knotting in half, allowing for the flap. Using the strong thread, sew the sides together.

7 CK the gold leather cord for 36 inches (91.4 cm). Find the center of the knotted cord and place it in the purse under the flap, just above the top of the purse front. With the strong thread, sew the cord to the inside back of the purse. Small stitches in and out of the CKs will not show. Fold the purse and sew up the sides.

8 LHK two 12-inch (30.5 cm) pieces of the thread to the middle of the wire. Push two threads through the hole in the bone from the front and two from the back. Bring the threads down and tie an OHK under the bone. Use these ends to thread through the fetishes and beads for the tassel.

FLOWER BROOCH

To create this brooch, you take a Clove Hitched strip knotted in a curve, draw it together, and embellish it with beads.

WHAT YOU DO

1 LHK one 28-inch (71.1 cm) cord onto the center section of the cotton roving. Repeat with another cord. Using outside left and right cords, tie a SK over the other two (filler) cords. Repeat with the rest of the cords.

2 Tape a tail from one of the yarn pieces out to the left. Tie VCHs across and back.

3 Draw a 5-inch (12.7 cm) circle on the paper and tape it to your board. Draw a vertical line through the center of the circle. You will use only the left side of the circle. Pin the knotting inside the line on the left side, starting at the top. As you knot, turn the board slightly and pin the knotting securely on the line. Keep the outside line pinned; it doesn't matter if the inside edge buckles a little.

4 As you VCH each row back and forth, leave a loop in the cord about ³⁄₈ inch (1 cm) in size every ³⁄₄ inch (1.9 cm) on the right side (inside). Each time you turn the cord on the left side, leave a loop no larger than ¹⁄₂ inch (1.3 cm). This produces a fringe on the outside of the brooch.

5 Knot to within an inch (2.5 cm) of the half-circle vertical line edge. End by making HCHs from left to right, leaving off the last two cords on the right. Continue leaving two cords off each time. When you finish, pull the left-hand filler cord toward the right, HCHing each cord in turn. As you knot each cord, pull it in to become a filler cord. Trim off two or three filler cords as you go, knotting over the ends. You should finish with eight cords. Tie an OHK to hold these cords in place.

TIP
Making this piece with a variegated yarn gives you a varied surface without having to knot in separate colors.

FINISHED LENGTH
2¹⁄₂ x 2¹⁄₂ inches (6.4 x 6.4 cm)

WHAT YOU NEED
8 red linen or cotton cords, each 28 inches (71.1 cm) in length

Red ¹⁄₄-inch-wide (6 mm) cotton roving, 6 inches (15.2 cm) in length

12 cords of red tape yarn, each 1¹⁄₂ yards (1.4 m) in length

Strong red thread and sewing needle

40 seed beads, size 6, in two tones of red

3 fan-shaped red/black CZ glass beads

2-inch (5.1 cm) diameter piece of red felt or leather

Pin back

KNOTS USED
LHK—Lark's Head Knot (page 112)

SK—Square Knot (page 114)

VCH—Vertical Clove Hitch (page 117)

HCH—Horizontal Clove Hitch (page 115)

OHK—Overhand Knot (page 113)

6 Cut off the excess roving on the right side. Thread a 1-yard (91.4 cm) piece of the strong thread through the needle and tie a knot on the end. Thread the needle through the loops on the right side, pulling tight and tying off. Overlap the ends and stitch them together with the same thread. Loose ends from the filler cords should hang out of the center. Thread seed beads on them.

7 Sew on the three CZ glass beads in the three flat areas, with the points facing the center. Cut off the excess cord at the other end of the roving. If the center of the roving is white, color it red with some paint. That point is the bottom of the brooch.

8 Make holes in the felt circle to push the pin ends through. Put the body of the pin under the felt. Add glue to the back of the brooch, place the pin back in place, and let it dry.

TIP
If you cannot find fan-shaped beads, long flat beads or rows of seed beads will work.

COPPER ZIGZAG

ADVANCED

This striking necklace combines copper beads and buttons on a multicolored cord knotted over with black linen. Making this project gives you great practice in developing a pattern with Horizontal Clove Hitches.

WHAT YOU DO

1 Thread the four black cords through the button toggle and double them up. With the outside left and outside right cords, SK over all the cords for 2 inches (5.1 cm). Thread the cords through the three discs. Pull the end of the 3-yard (2.7 m) cord through the three discs from underneath (the opposite way you pulled the cords through). Tie an OHK on the end of that cord to keep it from pulling out.

2 Pin the 3-yard (2.7 m) cord to the left side of the hanging cords to use as a filler cord. Starting with the black cord on the left, HCH each cord in turn over the filler cord. For the next row, pin the filler cord to the right and HCH to the left, slanting downward with about 1/2-inch (1.3 cm) gaps at the ends, forming a zigzag pattern. Continue for 4 inches (10.2 cm). Keep the necklace pinned to your board.

3 Thread four of the seed beads onto cords #2, #4, #6, and #7, counting from the left. HCH across the cords and beads in a straight line. Then HCH, allowing for a loop

on the outside edge. The side groups have five loops, the largest in the center (3/4 inch [1.9 cm]). Look at the pictured necklace for guidance. Curve the necklace slightly toward the center.

4 Bring all the cords together. With an outside left and an outside right cord, tie two SKs. Thread four cords through the copper button and tie three SKs. Do the zigzag pattern again for two loops as in step 2. Add another group of four seed beads and center seven loops. The largest loop should be 1 1/4 inches (3.2 cm) long. Repeat knotting with the seed beads.

5 Pin the necklace securely and reverse the board. To match the second side to the first as you knot, reverse the directions, making sure the second copper button is in line with the first. Continue until you add the three disc beads. Pull the 3-yard (2.7 m) cord through the discs along with all the cords. Trim the 3-yard (2.7 m) cord and finish as usual.

FINISHED LENGTH
24 inches (61 cm)

WHAT YOU NEED
4 black linen cords, each 4 yards (3.7 m) in length

Multicolored stiff round rayon cord, 3 yards (2.7 m) in length

Black toggle button

6 copper disc beads, 1/2 inch (1.3 cm) in diameter

16 copper seed beads, size 6

2 large copper buttons

KNOTS USED
SK—Square Knot (page 114)

HCH—Horizontal Clove Hitch (page 115)

OHK—Overhand Knot (page 113)

PRIMARY COLORS
Necklace
ADVANCED

This necklace gives you another chance to try the Cavandoli knotting used in the pendant on page 80, this time done in three bright colors. The pretty glass bead by Barbara Becker Simon holds it all together.

WHAT YOU DO

1 Thread three blue and three yellow cords through the toggle bar. Double up the cords. Using a blue cord on the left side and a blue on the right, SK for 2 inches (5.1 cm) over all the cords. Thread on one of the blue 5/8-inch (1.6 cm) beads.

2 Divide the cords into a blue group and a yellow group. Using a left and right cord in the blue group, HK for 3 inches (7.6 cm). Repeat with the yellow cords. Twist both knotted cords together. Tie all the cords in an OHK and thread them through the first round blue bead.

3 Spread the cords out, with the blue cords on the left and the yellow on the right. Using the rightmost yellow cord as a filler cord, HCH over it from left to right with each cord in turn. Place red seed beads on cords #2, #4, #7, and #9, counting from the left.

4 Using the right-hand cord as a filler cord, VCH five knots from right to left. Using the yellow cord as a filler, HCH two knots. Then tie one VCH with the yellow cord and two HCHs with the blue cord. Follow this pattern for 2 inches (5.1 cm).

5 Repeat step 3 using blue seed beads.

6 Gather all the cords together and thread them through one of the red 1/2-inch (1.3 cm) beads. Place the yellow cords on the left and the blue on the right. To introduce the red to that side of the necklace, tape a tail on the left with the 1 1/2-yard (1.4 m) cord and VCH from left to right and back. For the next row, tie six HCHs with the yellow cords over the red. Tie three rows and then two rows of VCHs with the red. Alternate three rows of each. Using the outside cords on left and the right, tie six HKs.

TIP
In making this necklace, you start at the back on each side and finish it in front.

FINISHED LENGTH
24 inches (61 cm)

WHAT YOU NEED
Cords of cotton, as follows:
6 cords of blue, each 3 yards
(2.7 m) in length
3 cords of yellow, each 3 yards
(2.7 m) in length
3 cords of red, each 3 yards
(2.7 m) in length
1–2 extra cords of each color,
1 1/2 yards (1.4 m) in length
Silver toggle set
2 large-holed 5/8-inch (1.6 cm) dark blue beads
2 round 1/2-inch (1.3 cm) blue beads
25–30 seed beads, size 6, in red, blue, and yellow
2 round 1/2-inch (1.3 cm) red beads
Round 3/4-inch (1.9 cm) yellow bead
Focal bead

KNOTS USED
SK—Square Knot (page 114)
HK—Half Knot (page 113)
VCH—Vertical Clove Hitch (page 117)
HCH—Horizontal Clove Hitch (page 115)
OHK—Overhand Knot (page 113)

7 Begin the other side of the necklace at the back. Using three red and three blue cords, repeat step 1, threading through the other part of the toggle. Thread on the second round blue bead.

8 Spread out the cords and arrange them from left to right: first blue, then red. Using the leftmost blue cord as a filler, HCH all cords over it. Thread cords #2, #5, #7, and #10 (counting from the left) through the yellow seed beads. Repeat a HCH.

9 Using the same filler cord, tie VCHs over all the cords, working from left to right and back. Begin a random pattern of knotting a red filler cord over the blue filler cord at various spots. Continue knotting for 2 inches (5.1 cm). If you need to, add in another 1½-yard (1.4 m) of blue cord.

10 Repeat step 8, using red seed beads. Thread all the cords through the round red bead. Lay out the cords from left to right: three blue, six red, and three blue.

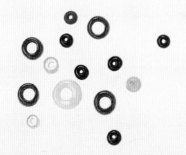

11 Using a 1½-yard (1.4 m) yellow cord, tie HCHs across to the right for the first row. Turn and knot four HCHs, a VCH (with yellow), two HCH, a VCH, and four HCHs to finish the second row. Use the following pattern to complete 14 rows:

Rows 3 and 4: Knot four HCHs, four VCHs, and four HCHs.

Rows 5 and 6: Knot HCHs across.

Rows 7 and 8: Knot four HCHs, four VCHs, and four HCHs.

Rows 9 and 10: Knot HCHs across.

Rows 11 and 12: Knot four HCHs, four VCHs, and four HCHs.

Row 13: Knot HCHs across.

Row 14: Knot four HCHs, a VCH, two HCHs, a VCH, and four more HCHs.

12 Tie six HKs. Pull all the cords from both sides through the round yellow bead. Tie an OHK with all the cords underneath the bead. Thread as many of the top cords from the top of the knot as possible through the focal bead. Then tie an OHK underneath. Thread on blue seed beads and trim at about 2 inches (5.1 cm). Let the other cords hang behind the focal bead. Tie two OHKs on these cords, trimming them off at 4 inches (10.2 cm).

FIBER RUFFLE
Necklace

ADVANCED

Based on a set of four triangles that open up to a three-dimensional shape, this design mixes three colors of your choice, all enhanced by tiny seed beads. You can easily double or triple the size of the necklace.

WHAT YOU DO

1 In the middle of your knotting board, lay the cords flat and close together in your selected color pattern. Leave a tail of 1 yard (91.4 cm) of all the cords coiled up and taped to the top left of your board. You will leave this tail taped down until you have finished the whole central section of the necklace. You will turn the board around as you knot each triangular section.

2 Let all the cords hang down straight on your board. HCH each cord over the left-hand cord (as a filler cord) in turn, working from left to right. Leave this cord hanging to the right. Repeat the HCH using the second cord on the left as a filler cord. Continue this pattern, tying HCHs over each subsequent cord on the left (as a filler cord), working to the right. You have now completed your first triangle.

3 For the second triangle, use the right-hand cords as filler cords while you knot toward the left. Turn your board clockwise and use the subsequent right-hand cords, in turn, as the filler cord.

4 To make the third triangle, turn your board to the left. Let the cords hang down and work from right to left. You will turn the board around as you knot each triangular section.

5 You will not have a complete square until you complete your fifth triangle, which you will knot partially over the top of the first triangle. Continue overlapping the triangles, pinning the triangles down through each layer. Complete 15 triangles. The 16th triangle must match the first. Knot it from left to right.

6 Undo the whole knotting and pin it down through all the layers to the top of the board, letting the cords hang down. Divide the cords on the left side into groups of six and seven cords. Choose two outer cords of the same color and HK over four filler cords for 2 inches (5.1 cm). Then change the color of the knots by choosing two cords of another color and HKing for 2 more inches (5.1 cm). Then change colors again. Repeat this step with the seven-cord group. If you run short of a color, add in a new 1-yard (94.1 cm) piece.

7 Roll and twist the two HKed cords together. Cut out the center cords, apply a dab of glue, and thread the cord through the first pony bead. Thread the cords through the necklace fastening and finish the knotting as usual. Repeat on the other side to complete.

FINISHED LENGTH
21 1/2 inches (54.6 cm)

WHAT YOU NEED
13 cords in three colors, each 3 1/2 yards (3.2 m) in length

2 pony beads

Fastening (hook and eyes)

KNOTS USED
HK—Half Knot (page 113)

HCH—Horizontal Clove Hitch (page 115)

DRUSY STONE
Necklace

EXPERIENCED

"Drusy" is a type of stone with a surface of tiny crystal formations similar to those found inside a geode. Here, the mossy tones of the stone are complemented by neutral background colors of beige and olive green.

WHAT YOU DO

FIRST LAYER

1 Draw out the overall size and shape of this necklace on the paper for your board.

2 Thread six cords of Color A (natural) through the toggle and double them up. With a left-hand cord and a right-hand cord, SK over all the cords for 2 inches (5.1 cm). Thread the cords through the large transparent bead. This necklace is knotted from the back down the left side (facing you on the board).

3 Use the outermost right-hand cord as a filler cord, and HCH from right to left. Thread four seed beads on cords #2, #5, #7, and #9, counting from the left. Repeat step 2, starting on the right.

4 Divide the cords into three groups of five cords. Tie HKs with the outer cords of each group. On the inside, tie 1¼ inch (3.2 cm) of knots. On the outer side, tie 1½ inch (3.8 cm) of knots. These knots start forming the curve of the necklace.

5 HCH each cord in turn over the left-hand cord as a filler cord. Thread on the cylinder bead with a cord from each side and repeat the HCH.

6 Divide the cords into three even groups. In the first group, with the left- and right-hand cords, tie three SKs. Repeat with the other two groups. Knot five rows of ASKs. Using the left-hand cord as filler, HCH over each cord in turn, from left to right and back.

TIP

The materials and instructions are listed by layer, which is how you construct this necklace. Add the yardage together to get the total yards needed.

FINISHED LENGTH
20 inches (50.8 cm)

WHAT YOU NEED
(First Layer)
9 cords of natural (Color A) linen, each 2 yards (1.8 m) in length

4 cords of green (Color B) cotton, each 2 yards (1.8 m) in length

3 cords of embroidery cotton in five colors, each 1½ yards (1.4 m) in length

Button toggle

2 transparent glass beads with large holes

8 seed beads, size 6

2 horn cylinder beads, ¾ inch (1.9 cm) in length

1 glass cube bead, ½ inch (1.3 cm) in length

A few small beads

¼-inch (6 mm) round bead

KNOTS USED
SK—Square Knot (page 114)

HK—Half Knot (page 113)

HCH—Horizontal Clove Hitch (page 115)

VCH—Vertical Clove Hitch (page 117)

OHK—Overhand Knot (page 113)

ASK—Alternating Square Knot (see step 3, page 43)

AHK—Alternating Half Knot (page 113)

AHH—Alternating Half Hitch (page 114)

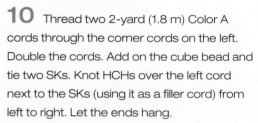

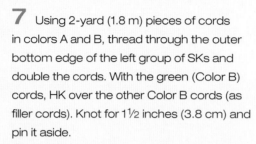

7 Using 2-yard (1.8 m) pieces of cords in colors A and B, thread through the outer bottom edge of the left group of SKs and double the cords. With the green (Color B) cords, HK over the other Color B cords (as filler cords). Knot for 1½ inches (3.8 cm) and pin it aside.

8 Using one color cord of the embroidery threads and the color B cord, tape a tail out to the left and begin VCH across all the cords from left to right. Add and drop colors at random or as desired. Thread in three seed beads. Curve the knotting to 1½ inches (3.8 cm) on the outside and 1¼ inches (3.2 cm) on the inside.

9 Bring down the ends of the knotted green cord on the left, pin them in place, and use them as filler cords under VCH knotting. Then HCH with each cord, picking up the hanging embroidery cords, enclosing them in the HCH. Leave the ends hanging to the right.

10 Thread two 2-yard (1.8 m) Color A cords through the corner cords on the left. Double the cords. Add on the cube bead and tie two SKs. Knot HCHs over the left cord next to the SKs (using it as a filler cord) from left to right. Let the ends hang.

11 Begin turning boards. LHK two more 2-yard (1.8 m) Color A cords onto the ends left hanging at the right. HCH all the hanging cords over the four cords on the left from step 10 (as filler cords), leaving a ½-inch (1.3 cm) gap in between the rows. Turn, pin, and make a series of five double rows of HCH spread out like a fan.

12 Repeat step 8, curving the knotting. The outer edge of the knotting should be 2¼ inches (5.7 cm), and the inside 1⅛ inch (2.8 cm). Thread in two small beads and turn your board.

13 HCH each cord in turn over the two cords on the right (as filler cords) from right to left. Thread on the small round bead. HCH back to the right.

14 Divide the cords from the left into three groups of four each. Leave the rest of the cords off to the right side. Tie six HKs with each group. Leave one cord out to each side. Tie five rows of ASKs.

15 Repeat step 5. Divide the cords into three groups of four again. With the two left groups, tie SKs for 1½ inches (3.8 cm). Tie AHHs with the third group.

16 Repeat step 3. Tie an OHK with all the cords. Cut out six cords. Thread on the second transparent bead. Finish the loop as usual.

SECOND LAYER

17 Begin again with the necklace right side up.

18 Cut the headpin to 1¼ inch (3.2 cm). Thread the frog onto the headpin and push it through the center of the VCH knotting on the right side. Coil up the headpin wire in the back.

19 Take the drusy stone pendant and glue on three hangers (page 13). Thread the 12-inch (30.5 cm) cords through each hanger and place on the center of the necklace. With the needle, pull the cords through the knotting to the back. On the back, tie an OHK with the two cords.

20 To form a "bezel" around the pendant, thread a small bead onto the filler cords you left hanging on the left. Add in a doubled 2-yard (1.8 m) cord in Color A. Using the outermost left and right cords, HK for 1 inch (2.5 cm). Pull the knotting toward the top of the pendant and continue knotting, enclosing the 12-inch (30.5 cm) cord ends left at the top. As you knot, thread an outside cord on the needle about every ¾ inch (1.9 cm) and pull the cord down under the edge of the pendant and up through the underneath of the knotting to secure it close to the edge of the pendant. Add in another cord if needed. Continue around the stone to the top and tie a SK with no fillers. Wind one long cord around the other cords for about 3 inches (7.6 cm). Pull it around the top end of the pendant and then under, gluing the end of the coil. Tie it off underneath the pendant and trim the ends.

21 Thread the loose filler cords on the right through the six fiber optic beads. Tie an OHK on the end and trim.

22 Thread two Color B cords through the needle and pull them through the cords between the two seed beads on the right side of necklace. Double up the cords and put two more cords on the other side. HH, using two cords on each side, for 1½ inches (3.8 cm). In turn, pull two cords from the left over the HCH and pull the remaining two cords under and up through the others. Tie a tight OHK with these four cords, repeating on the other side. Divide the cords into two groups of four cords, and SK for 2½ inches (6.4 cm). Weave in the knotting between the AHKs.

23 Pull the cords through the next set of HCH knots, adding in another 2-yard (1.8 m) cord in the center. Begin netting by tying five alternating rows of OHKs, leaving one cord out to the side as needed, tying five rows. Maintain about a ¼-inch (6 mm) space between the rows.

WHAT YOU NEED
(Second Layer)

Cords, as follows:
3 cords of linen in Color A,
    each 12 inches (30.5 cm) in length
4 cords of linen in Color A,
    each 2 yards (1.8 m) in length
3 cords of cotton in Color B,
    each 2 yards (1.8 m) in length

Headpin

Mother-of-pearl frog

Drusy stone pendant

Needle or wire needle

Several small beads

6 brown oval ½-inch (1.3 cm)
fiber optic beads

Crystal, 1 inch (2.5 cm) in length

Leaf agate

24 Upon reaching the pendant, after threading each cord in turn through the needle, bring the cord under the pendant and up through the HCHs on other side. Tie an OHK with each two cords and begin the netting again. As before, pull cords under and up through the next HCHs. Place the crystal on the VCHs and begin netting over it, making the spaces in the netting about ⅜ inch (1 cm) to hold the crystal tight.

25 Pull the cords through the two rows of HCHs. Tie an OHK with each two cords and divide them into two even groups. Using the outermost cords in the left group, tie 2 inches (5.1 cm) of SKs. Repeat with the other group. Pull the cords under the horn beads and up through. Tie AHHs with four cords on the left side for 1½ inches (3.8 cm). Tie an OHK at the end. Pull two cords over the HCHs and two under, tie another OHK, and trim the cords to ½ inch (1.3 cm). On the right side with the SKs, cut out all but one filler cord. Finish off the same as on the other side.

26 Trim off the remaining cords under the pendant, pulling any loose ends under the knotting. Save one cord, and thread it through the leaf agate, letting it hang just below the pendant. Tie it off underneath.

TIP
You probably won't find the exact beads I used, so be sure to balance the color pattern. Also, keep checking for even weight distribution so the necklace will hang evenly.

Knot Dictionary

As there are hundreds and hundreds of kinds of knots, how do you know which ones to learn? The knots I have selected here are the most widely used and important knots. They are used in maritime work, on farms, in lace making, and in many kinds of crafts.

By creating small, fine work, these same knots form beautiful patterns and textures. Each of these knots can be used in many different ways. Once you have mastered these, you may decide to venture out with some new ones. But all of the projects in this book have been made with these important knots (and a few variations).

Lark's Head Knot (LHK)

This is the primary knot for attaching your cords to a taut holding cord, a ring, a dowel, or a buckle. You can also use it to add in an additional doubled cord as you work.

1 To tie a LHK, fold your cord in half.

2 Pass the looped end of the cord behind the holding cord, from the top down.

3 Bring the loose ends of your cord over the holding cord and through the loop. Tighten.

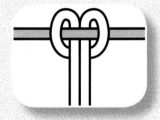

Reverse Lark's Head Knot (RLHK)

By knotting the opposite way, you can get subsequent knotting closer to the hanger (the dowel, cord, or ring holding the necklace). Whichever way you choose, be sure to tie all the knots in the same direction.

1 Pass the looped end of the folded cord behind the holding cord, from the bottom up.

2 Fold the loop over the holding cord and bring the loose ends through the loop. Pull to tighten.

Overhand Knot (OHK)

This knot is one of the few that can be made either with just one cord or with many. Use it to hold a bead in place, to take up slack, to keep beads from falling off the end of a cord, and to keep the ends of your cord from fraying. You can make it with many cords (as in making a tassel), or you can wrap it around other cords.

1 Make a loop.

2 Bring the end of the cord behind the loop and then out through the loop. Pull tight.

Half Knot (HK)

This is the first half of the Square Knot and is the same knot you use when tying your shoes. It must have at least one filler cord. You can tie it starting from the left or right—just remember to start it from the same side when you have to make a row of them. As you repeat this knot, it forms a perfect spiral. Just keep knotting and it will turn itself.

1 Bring the left cord over the filler cords to the right side.

2 Bring the right cord over the left cord, under the fillers, and over the left-side loop. Tighten.

Square Knot (SK)

Also known as the Flat Knot or Reef Knot, the Square Knot is probably the most familiar and widely used knot. It has many variations. The Greeks and Romans used this knot in paintings and sculptures. It is so strong, they referred to it as the Hercules Knot.

The Square Knot always remains flat and can have any number of filler cords. Also, the filler cords provide bulk to make your Square Knots thicker.

1 First, make a Half Knot.

2 Now bring the cord on the right over the filler cords and out to the left.

3 Bring the cord on the left over that cord, under the filler cords, and through the loop on the right. Tighten. The "bump" should be on the left.

4 Bring the cord on the right over that cord, under the filler cords, and through the loop on the left. Tighten. The little "bump" should be on the right side.

Half Hitch (HH)

The Half Hitch is the first half of the Clove Hitch Knot, just as the Half Knot is the first half of the Square Knot. It will not hold together on its own, but you can repeat it over and over, then end with an Overhand Knot. It makes a very decorative effect.

There are several versions of this knot, but for this book, we'll use it as a "hitch" or loop alternating from one cord to another. Thus, the instructions that follow are really to make an Alternating Half Hitch (AHH).

1 With two cords, either on their own and fastened down—or two cords from whatever project you are working on—make a single loop, one cord around the other.

2 Repeat this with the other cord around the first cord. Tighten.

3 Repeat each loop until you reach the desired length. If needed, tie an OHK to hold the AHH knot together.

Half Hitches are usually knotted around a third cord (see the Southwest Picot Choker on page 38). Notice, though, how this knot appears in the Ocean Wave Necklace (page 71). When you tie a HH around another cord, it creates a flat surface, whereas when you tie them around each other, it produces a cord-like effect.

Clove Hitch

This knot, also known as the Double Half Hitch, is probably the most useful and important of all knots. You can knot it in single rows going in any direction. With the rows knotted close together, it looks like a solid ribbed area with vertical or horizontal lines of knots. On the reverse side, another very pleasing pattern appears. You can use this pattern by knotting from the back with the necklace flipped over.

By holding the filler cord in different directions and knotting over it, you can develop curves, angles, rectangles, and more. I use the solid Clove Hitch often, sometimes knotting cotton embroidery threads over the filler cords to bring in an assortment of colors. (See the Versatile Brooch on page 65 for a clear example.).

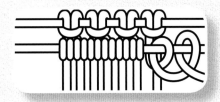

Horizontal Clove Hitch (HCH)

Make this knot over hanging cords that act as knotting cords over a filler cord. You can start this knot on either side or even in the middle.

1 Tape a 3-inch (7.6 cm) "tail" of filler cord—depending on how much knotting you intend to do, about 1½ yards (1.37 m) is a good working length—out to the left side of your work. Pin the tail to hold it securely.

2 Hold the filler cord across your work. Taking each hanging cord in turn, loop it twice around the filler cord and pull it tight. Loop it toward the left, but work toward the right. This produces a horizontal ridge.

Irina Serbina
*Leaves Necklace
(Macrame)*, 2003
19 5/8 inches (50 cm)
Nylon cord, aventurine,
hand-carved jade beads
Photo by artist

3 When you reach the right, place a pin at the end and pull the filler cord around the pin. Tie a HCH back to the left side.

4 When you reach the last knot, undo the tail and knot it in with the last cord. Keep knotting it in with the end cords until you have less than 1/2 inch (1.3 cm) of knotting. Trim the excess.

Sandy Swirnoff
Gallé: Green Trees, 2001
3 1/2 x 1 5/8 inches (9 x 4 cm)
Fiber, gallé glass shard,
seed beads, antique button
Photo by Melinda Holden

Ed Bing Lee
Oncidium: Everglades, 2001
6 1/2 x 4 x 1/2 inches
(16.5 x 10.1 x 1.2 cm)
Linen, cotton
Photo by John Woodin

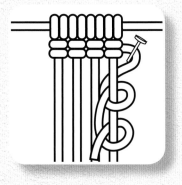

Vertical Clove Hitch (VCH)

To tie the Vertical Clove Hitch, reverse the filler cord and knotting cords.

1 Tape the "tail" of your cord out to the left. This cord is now the cord showing, as opposed to the cord you added for the HCH, which became the filler cord that the knotting covered.

2 Make the knotted loops vertically across each of the hanging filler cords. Bring the knotting cord under the hanging cord, and then make the loops. Tighten.

3 When you reach the right side, loop around a pin and knot back to the left.

If you do not want to add an extra cord to work with, use the left- or right-hand cord as either the filler cord or the knotting cord.

Irina Serbina
*Yellow Jade Rose Necklace
(Macrame)*, 2002
17 3/4 inches (45 cm)
Nylon cord, hand-carved
yellow jade
Photo by artist

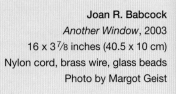

Joan R. Babcock
Another Window, 2003
16 x 3 7/8 inches (40.5 x 10 cm)
Nylon cord, brass wire, glass beads
Photo by Margot Geist

Useful Techniques

In the sections that follow, we'll go beyond the basic knots to cover many of the techniques you'll need to work with cords, knots, and beads.

Binding Knot (BK) or Whipping

When you're ready to tie a group of cords together, use an Overhand Knot (page 113). There is, however, a much neater-looking knot you can make by binding or whipping a separate cord around the loose cords.

1 Turn the knotted piece over and begin at the back.

2 With a 10-inch (25.4 cm) piece of cord, make a loop about ¾ inch (1.9 cm) on the end of the cord and hold it with your thumb.

3 Wind the other end of the cord around the cords and over the loop.

4 Run the end of the cord through the loop and then pull the other end. The top end is enclosed in the coil. Tighten.

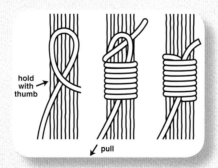

5 Put a dab of glue on the end before pulling it inside to make sure it holds. Trim the ends.

Ending Knots for Cord Ends

Tying knots (or beads with knots) onto the hanging end of a cord gives a more finished appearance. The Figure 8 (shown above) and the Overhand Knot (page 113) give you two choices for securing the end of a cord.

Cord Lengths

For the projects in this book, I have worked out the lengths of cord you will need. Of course, the amount you need varies with tension—how tightly or loosely you tie the knots. I strive for a firm knot, but not one that is pulled very tight. If you use a thicker or thinner cord, the amount you need will also vary. Always figure that you'll need a little extra cord.

When creating my jewelry, I never worry about what lengths of cord to use. Unless I am working on something very small, such as earrings or bracelets, I start with a 3½-yard (3.2 m) piece of cord. Doubling this length gives me a 1¾-yard (1.6 m) length, which is approximately the amount I can easily pull out to the end of my arm. If you run short or need additional cords, you can add them in very easily.

Here's a tip that will allow you to save on the cord you use: As you knot, remember that after you thread on a bead, you can switch knotting cords. Pick the longest cords to work with. This helps keep all your cords roughly the same length. This tip also reduces the need to add in new cords as some become too short.

Adding and Subtracting Cord

In the process of knotting, you'll find times when you need to add a cord to your design or take a cord out. Plan ahead as you knot. You will begin to spot the places where you can add a new cord for a shortened one and you can cut out a cord that's too long. Of course, if you work a project more than once, you will know to lengthen or shorten the cords as needed. The following sections give step-by-step advice on adding regular and filler cords, and removing a cord when necessary.

Adding a Cord

1 Use a Lark's Head Knot (LHK) to add two more cords (one cord doubled), knotting it around a single cord or group of cords that lay horizontally in the knotting. Use it as a separate layer of cords by hooking over the first layer of LHKs. For an example, see the Showcase Pendant on page 78.

2 Use a tapestry needle to pull a length of cord through the section where you need additional cords. See Three Squares Necklace (page 33) and Double Donuts (page 68) for examples.

Joan R. Babcock
Untitled, 1999
16 x 3 ½ inches (40.5 x 9 cm)
Nylon cord, marquesite stone,
glass beads
Photo by Hawthorne Studios

Irina Serbina
*Rose Quartz Flower Necklace
(Macrame)*, 2003
16 ½ inches (42 cm)
Nylon cord, rose quartz,
hand-carved
flower and beads
Photo by artist

Sandy Swirnoff
Water Over Rocks, 2006
3 ⅜ x 2 ½ inches
(8.5 x 6.5 cm)
Fiber, old Tibetan turquoise,
Tibetan turquoise
melon bead, pyrite
Photo by Peter Lee

Joan R. Babcock
Tibetan Bells, 2004
$11\,^3/_4$ x $3\,^7/_8$ inches (30 x 10 cm)
Nylon cord, brass, silver
Photo by Margot Geist

Irina Serbina
Mother of Pearl Inlaid Donut Necklace, 2004
$17\,^3/_4$ inches (45 cm)
Nylon cord, mother-of-pearl
Photo by artist

Sandy Swirnoff
Pods, 2003
$2\,^3/_4$ x $3\,^1/_8$ inches (7 x 8 cm)
Fiber, serpentine pendant,
serpentine carved flowers,
vintage glass, seed beads
Photo by Melinda Holden

Adding Filler Cords

1 If you are knotting Horizontal Clove Hitches and your filler cord becomes too short, lay another cord along with it, leaving a "tail," and knot over both cords for 1 inch (2.5 cm).

2 Then trim the tail of the new cord and cut out the old cord.

This method works with Square Knotting and Vertical Clove Hitching as well, if you find a filler cord is running too short.

Taking a Cord Out

The first place to be concerned about getting rid of cords is at the end. Before threading on that last pony bead, you will likely need to eliminate some cords, as the ending knots require the cords to be doubled, which would make the knotting thicker at the end than the knotting at the beginning. Unless the cords are very thin, cut out all but four, making sure not to cut the knotting cords. (See Ending Knots for Cord Ends on page 118.)

Tie an Overhand Knot and cut out some of the cords. With Half Knots or Square Knots, you can cut out some of the filler cords. If the ending cord is a Vertical Clove Hitch, you can pull two cords together and knot them as one cord. With the Horizontal Clove Hitch, you can knot over two or more cords together. (See the instructions for the Showcase Pendant on page 78.)

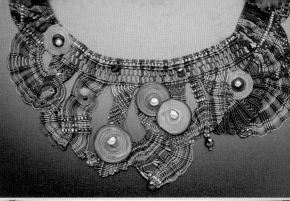

Sandy Swirnoff
Coming Full Circle, 2000
4 1/2 x 1 5/8 inches (11.5 x 4 cm)
Fiber, glass discs, seed beads,
pearls, antique nail heads
Photo by Melinda Holden

Sometimes you want a flat, sealed-off ending, especially when knotting a small item like an earring or pendant. Cut the cords off, leaving a 1/2-inch (1.3 cm) end. Fold it back and glue it down. Then, you can also glue on a piece of felt or leather to cover them. (See the Yellow Earrings with Beaded Fringe [page 64] and Autumn Gold Purse [page 92] projects for examples of this.)

Another trick is to pull an extra random single cord to the back, weaving it under an available loop. Glue it down and cut it off.

Working with Beads

There are so many kinds of beads—different shapes, sizes, and holes, not to mention the various hole sizes—that you should learn a few basic ways to use them in your work. Here are some tips and techniques that will help as you use beads.

Enlarging a Bead Hole

Do not allow your work to be hampered by the size of a bead hole! Sometimes you need to enlarge a hole so that all the cords you are using will pass through it. First check the hole to see if can be enlarged. Beads made of wood, shell, nuts, seed, bone, and ivory often have a rough surface within the hole that you can easily file away with a round jewelry file. These materials are also easy to drill. When drilling, I use an old adjustable pair of pliers to hold the bead. Put tape over the rough edges of the pliers to protect the bead, if necessary. Be careful if you try to drill a plastic bead, as the heat from the drill can melt the plastic and ruin the drill bit.

Kris Buchanan
Freeform Macrame, 2006
16 x 3 1/2 x 3/4 inches
(40.5 x 9 x 2 cm)
Cord, fiber beads,
lampworked beads
Beads by Sharon Peters
Photo by artist

Irina Serbina
Blue Cocktail Purse, 2004
6 3/4 x 4 7/8 inches (17 x 12.5 cm)
Nylon cord, lapis lazuli, silk
Photo by artist

Ed Bing Lee
Striped Masdevallia, 2001
2 x 4 x 1/2 inches
(5.2 x 10.1 x 1.3 cm)
Linen, cotton
Photo by John Woodin

Irina Serbina
Tiger Eye Donut Necklace, 2002
17 3/4 inches (45 cm)
Nylon cord, tiger eye bead
Photo by artist

Smoothing a Bead Hole

Glass beads often have a rough interior surface that can inadvertently cut a cord. You can file and sandpaper these surfaces to smooth them out.

Using Tape Hole

If you are having trouble forcing cords through a bead hole, try placing a small piece of cellophane tape on the ends of the cords. Sometimes the slicker surface of the tape will allow you to push the cords through the bead and pull them through from the other side, with pliers if necessary. When using this technique, wrap the tape so it tapers to a point at the end of the cords.

Using Glue

You can put white glue on cord ends to stiffen them. This will also keep the ends from fraying. If you're hesitant about using white glue in your jewelry, try just wetting the cord ends. Sometimes this simple trick does the job.

Squeezing the Cords

If you have to thread multiple cords, first try to get just two of them through the bead. Then, one at a time, place another cord between the two threaded cords and squeeze it through the bead hole.

Using Needles

This is another alternative for threading cords. You can pull cords through a bead hole with a beading needle or a thin doubled-up wire. Keep these items handy, as you will find many times that you have to thread a cord in and out again.

Embedding Wire

If any of these methods don't work, you can still use the bead. If you can't widen the hole or thread any of your cords through the bead, try imbedding a jewelry wire in the cord. For an example, see the Carved Stone Pendant on page 74.

Using Flat Beads

If a bead is flat or has a flat side, just continue the cords along the back of the bead. For example, see the Southwest Picot Choker (page 38) and Double Donuts (page 68). An alternative is to run one or two cords through the bead, and then tie Half Knots (HK) with the remaining cords around the bead on one side, picking up the cords running through the beads on the other side. Then you can continue with your design. As a variation, divide the remaining cords in half, and HK or SK (Square Knot) around the bead on both sides. To see a project with two beads added on the outside cords with the filler cords straight, check out the Stylishly Hemp Necklace on page 36.

If you're working with flat beads, there is another possibility. To make the bead lie flat, thread one cord over the top and down through the center hole. Thread another up from underneath and over. Carry the other cords along the back and bring them all together with a SK just past the bead. You can also SK the cords underneath the flat bead. See Stones, Bones & Fossils (page 88) for an example.

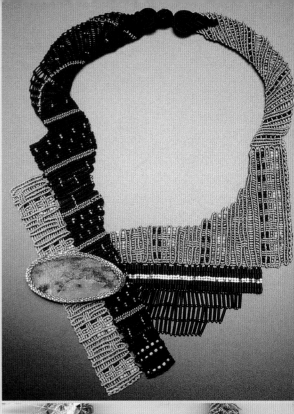

Sandy Swirnoff
Daum: Japanese Autumn, 2001
2⅞ x 3¾ inches (7.3 x 9.5 cm)
Nylon, silk, Daum glass shard,
vintage and Japanese seed beads
Photo by Peter Lee

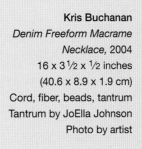

Kris Buchanan
*Denim Freeform Macrame
Necklace,* 2004
16 x 3½ x ½ inches
(40.6 x 8.9 x 1.9 cm)
Cord, fiber, beads, tantrum
Tantrum by JoElla Johnson
Photo by artist

Kris Buchanan
*Blue & Purple Freeform Macrame
Necklace,* 2006
16 1/2 x 4 x 3/4 inches
(41.9 x 10.2 x 1.9 cm)
Cord, fiber, beads, tantrum
Tantrum by JoElla Johnson
Photo by artist

Ed Bing Lee
Paphiopedilum: Cooksbridge
2001
4 x 3 x 1 inches
(10.1 x 7.6 x 2.5 cm)
Linen, cotton
Photos by John Woodin

Using Headpins

Another way to put flat disks on your jewelry is to thread a headpin through the hole and make a loop in the back. Then the cords go through the loop. If you want to add on a flat bead—or any bead—afterwards in a Clove Hitched area, thread the bead on a 1 1/2-inch (3.8 cm) headpin. Push the headpin through the knotting. On the back, make a wound-up coil. Bend the coil over and flatten it against the back of the knotting.

Using Seed Beads

You can add seed beads on rows of outside cords or inside cords. Look through the projects in this book for examples, such as the Funky Ceramic Bead Necklace (page 40). The largest size seed bead (#6) works best with this type of jewelry.

Holding the Beads

If the holes in your beads are too large, tie an overhand knot (OHK) before and after the bead to hold it in place. You can also thread a smaller bead (or a seed bead) on either side of the large bead to help block up the hole. A third possibility is to thread on a long cylinder bead or a row of seed beads that will fit inside the larger bead.

About the Author

Jane Olson-Phillips has worked as an interior decorator and public school teacher. Her work has been featured in several books and magazines including *Beadwork* and *Belle Armoire*. After receiving a B.A. in Fine Arts from the University of Connecticut, she continued her studies—both in this country and in England, where she lived for many years—in silversmithing, basketry, weaving, ceramics, and etching. She has taught arts and crafts to both adults and children, and has exhibited and sold original artwork. She has traveled to many countries, collecting the unusual beads, fossils, stones, and knotted objects that appear in her collections and her work. She designs fiber jewelry that is influenced by her travels and includes her own polymer clay work.

Affiliations:

Beadesigner International
The Bead Society of Greater Washington, D.C.
The Bead Society of Great Britain
Baton Rouge Bead Society
Centre for Bead Research
The Bead Study Trust of the UK

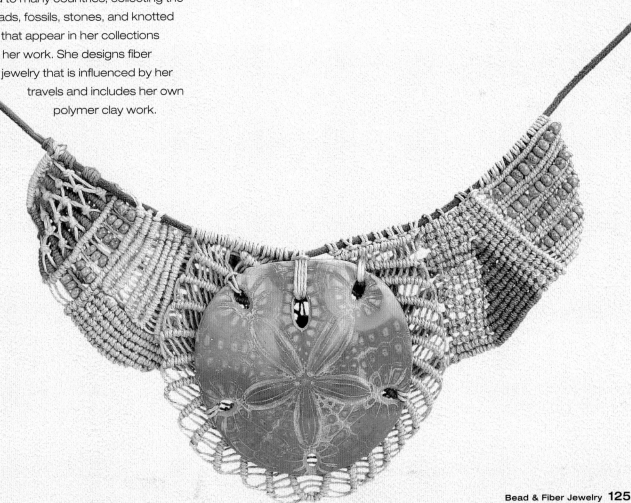

ACKNOWLEDGMENTS

Thanks to my husband, Wilton Phillips, for his support, and to Susie Blyskal for her "knotting checks." I'd also like to thank the folks at Lark Books, including editors Terry Taylor, Larry Shea, and Mark Bloom. And while I never met Dana Irwin, I wish to thank her for making the book look so wonderful!

A NOTE ON SUPPLIERS

Usually, you can find the supplies you need for making the projects in Lark books at your local craft supply store, discount mart, home improvement center, or retail shop relevant to the topic of the book. Occasionally, however, you may need to buy materials or tools from specialty suppliers. In order to provide you with the most up-to-date information, we have created a listing of suppliers on our website, which we update on a regular basis. Visit us at www.larkbooks.com, click on "Sources," and then search for the relevant materials. You can also search by book title, vendor, and author name. Additionally, you can search for supply sources located in or near your town by entering your zip code. You will find numerous companies listed, with the web address and/or mailing address and phone number.

INDEX